EAST ASIAN CULTURAL STUDIES SERIES, No. 10

AN INTRODUCTION TO VIETNAMESE CULTURE

NGUYỄN KHẮC KHAM

THE CENTRE FOR EAST ASIAN CULTURAL STUDIES
TOKYO

c/o The Toyo Bunko
Honkomagome 2-chome, 28-21, Bunkyo-ku
Tokyo, Japan

This book is Published with
the Assistance of UNESCO, in Implementation of
the Major Project on
Mutual Appreciation of Eastern and Western Cultural Values.

Editor: Kazuo ENOKI
Deputy Director
The Centre for East Asian Cultural Studies

Printed by
TOKYO PRESS CO., LTD.
Itabashi, Tokyo, Japan

EAST ASIAN CULTURAL STUDIES SERIES
No. 10

AN INTRODUCTION TO VIETNAMESE CULTURE

Nguyễn Khắc Kham is Associate Professor and Head of the Department of Vietnamese Language and Writing, Faculty of Letters, University of Saigon and Director of the Directorate of National Archives and Libraries of the Republic of Vietnam. Born in Hanoi in 1910, he graduated from the University of Paris. Since 1956, he has served in the cultural activities of the government and is now Secretary-General of Vietnamese National Commission for Unesco. He has published several books and articles on Vietnamese culture, especially on language and literature (see Bibliography). He has attended several international conferences including the XXVIth International Congress of Orientalists held in New Delhi in 1964.

Already published

EAST ASIAN CULTURAL STUDIES SERIES:

1/2. The Formation of Modern Japan as viewed from Legal History, by Kichisaburo Nakamura, 1962.
3. East Asia in Old Maps, by Hiroshi Nakamura, 1962.
4. Industrialization of Japan, by Ichiro Nakayama, 1963.
5. A Short History of Korea, compiled by the Centre for East Asian Cultural Studies, 1963.
6/7. The Role of Hong Kong in the Cultural Interchange between East and West, by Lo Hsiang-lin, 1963-64. 2 vols.
8. Chulalongkorn the Great, by Prachoom Chomchai, 1965.
9. The Thirteenth Dalai Lama, by Tokan Tada, 1965.
11. Literary Debates in Modern China, 1918-1937, by Amitendranath Tagore, 1967.

PREFACE

Early in 1964, I submitted to the XXVIth International Congress of Orientalists held in New Delhi a paper entitled *Vietnamese Studies and Their Relationships to Asian Studies.* I had for purpose to deal with interrelationships and mutual contributions of Vietnamese and Asian cultures.

Later on, at the request of the Centre for East Asian Cultural Studies in Tokyo, I have added new chapters especially on the impact of Western cultures.

This book, resulting from the above enlargement, attempts to show how Vietnamese culture has preserved its distinctive originality in spite of many cultural patterns stemming from other cultures of the East and the West.

Effectively, in successive contacts with Austro-Asiatic, Indian, Chinese and Western cultures, Vietnamese culture has taken some elements from those foreign cultures, while rejecting other ones. This process testifies to the pre-existence of an indigenous culture or, at least, a peculiar Vietnamese mental attitude which must have played a decisive role in this cultural selectivity. At the same time, it may throw much more light on the mechanism of trans-culturation as well as of neo-culturation. Furthermore, it proves to be of the utmost interest for Orientalists in the field of cultural anthropology, the more so because most of Asian cultures are now undergoing a grave crisis originated from their contact with such cultures as basically opposed to their traditional spirit.

Frankfurt am Main
January 1967

Nguyễn Khắc Kham

ACKNOWLEDGEMENTS

I deem it my duty to extend my deep gratitude to Dr. Naoshiro Tsuji, Director of the Centre for East Asian Cultural Studies for his personal encouragement I have been given.

I also gratefully credit Prof. Kazuo Enoki, Deputy Director of the Centre for his suggestions concerning the enlargement of my paper submitted to the XXVIth International Congress of Orientalists.

Finally, I would like to express my sincere thanks to Mr. Shigeru Ikuta for many improvements of my manuscript and for the pertinent rearrangement he has kindly made of some chapters.

Nguyen Khac Kham

CONTENTS

LIST OF ILLUSTRATIONS

NOTE ON VIETNAMESE PRONUNCIATIONS

Vietnamese writing system, that is called Quốc-ngũ', is used to represent Vietnamese proper nouns in this book.

There are two kinds of diacritic marks; that which represents tones and that which represents variations of vowel. Six tones are represented as follows: a (mid trailing pitch), à (low trailing), ả (mid-low dropping), ã (rising, accompanied by glottal stop), á (high rising), ạ (low dropping, accompanied by glottal stop). "'" (of o' and u') represents unroundness, "^" (of â, ê, and ô) is used to represent the narrow variation, and "˘" (of ă denotes the shortness. Two diacritics, sometimes, fall on the same vowel, e.g. Nguyễn, Trần, Đặng.

Alphabets of Quốc-ngũ' are usually pronounced as in English with the exceptions as follows.

Đ (đ) is pronounced like *d* in English. D, gi, and r are pronounced like *z* in English *zoo* (in Saigon dialect, d and gi are pronounced somewhat like *y* in English *yes,* and r like *r* in English). S and x are pronounced like *s* in English (in Saigon dialect s is pronounced like English *sh*). Both ch and tr are pronounced like English *ch* (in Saigon dialect, tr is pronounced somewhat like English *tr* in *try*).

When h is used in digraphs or trigraph, such as: ch,

gh, kh, ngh, nh, ph and th, (a) in th and kh, it represents aspiration, (b) ch, nh and ph are pronounced respectively as English *ch,* French *gn* and *f,* and (c) in gh and ngh which stand before i, ê and e, it denotes that g or ng is not palatalized by these front vowels (e.g. gh in ghi is the same with the initial consonant in ga).

CHAPTER I

GEOGRAPHICAL AND HISTORICAL BACKGROUND

Lying between 8°33′ and 23°22′ north latitude, Vietnam is bounded on the west by Cambodia and Laos, on the south by the Gulf of Siam, and on the east by the Pacific Ocean which washes her coast along some 1,460 miles. On account of her privileged geographical position in Southeast Asia, she has always been a crossroad of many important ethnic migrations and main streams of various civilizations. Vietnam originally comprised North Vietnam and the northern part of Central Vietnam. Conquered by China in 111 B.C., she remained under the influence of Chinese culture for the following ten centuries. Independent again in 939 A.D., she then entered on a struggle for influence with Champa, which she finally absorbed in 1471. Soon the Vietnamese were masters of the eastern part of the Indochinese Peninsula from the basin of the Red River to the lower Mekong.

The first traces of human life on Vietnam's territory date back to about the end of the Tertiary period and consist of pieces of stone either left in their natural shapes and serving as rudimentary tools or worked into pointed spears or sharp blades. At the end of the palaeolithic era and the beginning of mesolithic era, were used other kinds of tools also made of stone but shaped into such weapons as hatches, gouges, adzes, paring-knives, and arrowheads. The people who used these tools lived in limestone caverns on the right bank of the Red River, and left abundant evidence of their industry mostly in Hòa-bình. Hence the name "Hoabinian culture" which dates back to about 3000 B.C. Hòa-bình's cut-stone implements were frequently found together with tools made of polished stone which were unearthed mostly at Bắc-so'n. The culture of this second prehistoric period was named Bacsonian culture which dates back to about 1000 B.C. The former was supposed to be used by the people of Melanesian stock and the latter by the people of Indonesian extraction. In the neolithic era, about the first millenary B.C., the Austro-Asiatic culture spread over Vietnam. Its characteristic elements are ready-made stone axes to be fitted with handles. Megalithic works at Xuân-lộc also belong to the Austro-Asiatic culture. However, the Bacsonian culture progressed on the spot until the introduction of metal from about 500 B.C. to the approach of the Christian Era. It was not before the middle of the first century A.D. that the Bacsonian culture was destroyed in North Vietnam by the Chinese invasion, but it still remained preserved in some Indochinese mountains and in Southeast Asia. Then came the period of Dongsonian culture.

At that time, China, which had just come out of the

Bronze age, conquered North Vietnam for colonization. Local cultivations were suddenly reactivated by the techniques brought by the Chinese conquerors. These techniques were not at all of Chinese origin, but imported from a vast area which included southwestern China, the population of which was not solely Chinese. Thus at Đông-so'n in Thanh-hóa province were discovered, at the same spots, iron objects, bronze works such as vases and drums and many polished tools as well as others in cut stone. These finds show clearly that the Dongsonian culture was a blend of local traditions, both technical and aesthetic. That is why there could be found such Chinese objects as swords, vases, bronze mirrors and such bronze objects of Indonesian origin as weapons of various models, lamps, drums with indigenous form.

During the Chinese colonization which lasted ten centuries, many settlers arrived in North Vietnam. The result was a blend of races in which the Mongolian element tended to become progressively the most important one. The arrival of the Chinese led to the exodus of North Vietnam's Indonesian populations toward the mountainous regions of Indochina and the islands of Southeast Asia. The Muongs, the Moïs, the Indonesians of Borneo and Sumatra are their descendants. The ancestors of the present Indonesians were able to bring along with them the vestiges of ancient cultures. This explains the analogy between the decorative motifs used by the Dayak of Borneo and those found on bronze drums of the Dongsonian period.

It is also in the course of the Bronze age that appeared the legendary dynasty of Hồng Bàng. According to Vietnamese legends, corroborated by Chinese annals, the Viets (Yüeh), ancestors of the Vietnamese, were once included in the kingdom of Xích Quỷ which was bounded on the north by Hunan province, on the south by Champa, on the west by Szechwan and on the east by the South China Sea. At the end of the third century B.C., the Lạc Việt (Lo Yüeh), one of Xích Quỷ kingdom's Việt tribes, in their southward move reached the Red River where they established Văn Lang kingdom over which reigned the dynasty of Hồng Bàng.

Later on, the kingdom of Văn Lang was replaced by the kingdom of Âu Lạc. Its first king was Thục Vu'o'ng Phán. It succumbed in 207 B.C. to the Chinese General Chao T'o (Triệu Dà) who established the kingdom of Nam Việt with its capital at Phiên-ngung (Fan-yü; now Canton), thus founding the dynasty of the Triệu. In 111 B.C., General Lu Po-tê was sent to Nam Việt by Emperor Wu Ti of Chinese Han dynasty to overthrow the Triệu and to make Nam Việt a Chinese province called Giao-chỉ (Chiao Chih), which literally meant *toes crossed*.

This was the beginning of the first Chinese domination which lasted until 39 A.D., when Tru'ng Trắc and her younger sister, Tru'ng Nhị raised their own troops against the Chinese authorities. After fighting victoriously, they proclaimed themselves queens, and reigned over all the country from their new capital established at Mê-linh.

But their reign lasted only four years before the Chinese armies under the command of Ma Yüan returned to impose their protectorate anew. The second Chinese domination (43–544) was marked by memorable accomplishments of such Chinese governors as Hsi Kuang (Tích Quang), Jên Yen (Nhâm Diên) and Shih Hsieh (Sĩ Nhiếp) in the field of the propagation of Chinese culture in Vietnam. In 544, under favour of a weakened Chinese authority, a Vietnamese kingdom called Vạn Xuân was established. However, for more than a half century there followed a very confused period in which transitory dynasties by turn contested for power. The third Chinese domination (603–938) came as a result of the rivalries of the Vietnamese dynasties and a reassertion of Chinese power. In 605, the Chinese General Liu Fang (Lu'u Phu'o'ng) launched an expedition against Champa and in 679 the Chinese protectorate was established over what became later Central Vietnam. In 863, invaders from Nan Chao kingdom in Yunnan swept down and occupied the country briefly before being repulsed by the Chinese Governor Kao P'ien (Cao Biền) in 866. In 906, under favour of the diminishing of Chinese power, the Chinese governor was replaced by the first Vietnamese governor, Khúc Thù'a Dụ and finally, in 938, Ngô Quyền, after defeating the Chinese forces at the Bạch-đằng River, completely freed Vietnam from Chinese suzerainty.

Under this long Chinese protectorate which lasted more than ten centuries, Vietnam was being deeply influenced by Chinese civilization. Before the Chinese domination ended, there appeared a typically Vietnamese culture in North Vietnam. Its vestiges were found in Đại-la, the capital which Kao P'ien built in the northwestern part of Hanoi around 864; hence the name Đại-la culture which incorporates all three influences of Indian, Chinese and Dongsonian cultures. The most characteristic art works of this culture are represented by small six-tiered stupas with figures of Buddha carved on each tier and with slightly curved roofs that suggest the architecture of houses as figured on Dongson bronze drums.

After the first three national dynasties which had only a short period of existence, it was the Lý dynasty that remained in power for more than two centuries from 1010 to 1225. Under this dynasty, Chinese attacks were successfully fought back and two provinces of Champa, Quảng-bình and Quảng-trị, were annexed to Vietnam.

As Buddhism flourished at that time, many Buddhist pagodas were built. In addition to works of architecture, the Lý dynasty also left famous pieces of celadon. The kilns used for the production of these remarkable items were found mostly in Thanh-hóa province; hence the name Thanh-hóa's celadon wares. The Lý were succeeded by the Trần dynasty (1225–1400). It was during this period that the national script of Chữ'-nôm was used for the first time in literary field and the first annals of Vietnam, Đại-Việt sử'-ký, were published. While cultural development was going on, many feats of arms were recorded. Three times successively, the Mongol hordes of Kublai Khan invaded the country, but were turned back and finally they were cut to pieces on the Bạch-đằng River by the Vietnamese troops under the leadership of General Trần Hu'ng-đạo. The Trần also proved their skill in diplomacy by adding two more Cham districts to the national territory in 1306 through the marriage of Princess Huyền Trân with Prince Harijit who later became King of Champa under the royal title of Jaya Simhavarman III. In 1400, the Trần dynasty was put to an end by Hồ Quý Ly's usurpation. Under favour of internal disorders following the Hồ's accession to the throne, Vietnam fell again under the Chinese yoke in the form of the Ming domination (1407–27). As the Ming planned a long stay in the country, they tried by various means to carry out their Vietnam assimilation policy. Public education was to be given in Chinese. The Chinese classics were substituted for the Vietnamese ones which were collected and sent to Chin-ling (now Nanking). Fortunately, the Ming domination was short-lived. As early as 1418, a centre of resistance was organized by Lê Lọ'i in his own native village of Lam-so'n in Thanh-hóa province and finally in 1427, the Ming rule was brought to an end after Lê Lọ'i's victory at Chi-lăng. In commemoration of the recovering of national independence Lê Lọ'i instructed Nguyễn Trãi to write a proclamation entitled Bình Ngô đại cáo, which is considered as a masterpiece of political literature under the Lê dynasty.

Establishing his capital at Đông-kinh (Hanoi) and

re-naming his kingdom Đại Việt or the Great Việt, Lê Lọ'i took the royal title of Lê Thái-tồ (1428–33). Among Lê Lọ'i's successors, we should insist on Lê Thánh-tôn (1460–97). Under his reign, Vietnam knew one of the most prosperous periods of her history. The country was administratively reorganized. The tax regime was revised. A population census was made every six years. The king took so great an interest in agriculture that he appointed special officials for promoting cultivation and exploitation of abandoned lands. He reacted strongly against the loose morality of his time. The famous Hồng-đú'c legal code was promulgated under his reign between 1470 and 1497. In the literary field, an administrative map of the country was drawn up and a fifteen-volume history of Đại Việt was written by Ngô Sĩ Liên by the king's order. Lê Thánh-tôn himself was a great poet and writer. He was the author of Quỳnh-uyển củ'u-ca (*Royal Anthology*) and Thân-chinh Ký-sụ' (*War Memories*). He also headed the Academy of Letters named Tao-đàn. Among other numerous cultural accomplishments, the Lê dynasty, especially Lê Thánh-tôn's reign, has left in Lam-so'n several tombs whose gravestones mounted on stone turtles summarize all the traditional arts of Vietnam. The army was also reorganized under Lê Thánh-tôn and was credited with many victories and with increasing Đại Việt's prestige abroad. In 1470, Lê Thánh-tôn personally led an expedition against Champa. After laying hold of this country, he divided it into three parts each under a local lord. As for the districts of Đồ-bàn, Đại-chiêm and Cổ-lũy, they were merged in a new province of Quảng-nam under the direct rule of the king.

After Lê Thánh-tôn's death in 1497, the Lê dynasty fell into a period of decline. In the first half of the sixteenth century, Vietnam was partitioned between the two rival dynasties. It was the Mạc, the usurping dynasty known as the Northern Court that ruled the territory from So'n-nam to the north. The territory from Thanh-hóa to the south was ruled by the Nguyễn who was known as the Southern Court. In 1592 Trịnh Sâm succeeded in restoring the Lê dynasty in the north after removing the usurper. However, Vietnam continued to be partitioned between the two great rival families. The Trịnh seized real powers in the north with nominal rule of Lê kings. At the same time, the Nguyễn settled as independent lords in the south. During the Trịnh-Nguyễn internecine war, the whole coastal area up to the southernmost extremity of Indochinese peninsula was added by the Nguyễn to national territory. It was also during this period that Western missionaries and, later on, traders successively arrived for the first time in Vietnam.

At the end of the eighteenth century, the uprising of the Tây-so'n brothers put an end to the Trịnh-Nguyễn internecine war and to the Lê dynasty. Vietnam was divided between the three Tây-so'n brothers. But the unity of the Tây-so'n began to break up in 1786. Profiting by this disunity, Nguyễn Ánh, a descendant of the Nguyễn lords, succeeded in recovering the lands of his forefathers in the south, and later on, in putting the north under his control. In 1802, he proclaimed himself Emperor Gia-long, changing the name of the country from An Nam into Việt Nam and establishing his capital at Phú-xuân (now Huế) in Central Vietnam. Gia-long and most of his successors were indefatigable architects. Marvellous buildings such as the Imperial Palace, the imperial tombs in Huế as well as citadels and fortresses scattered all over the country testify to a very flourishing art. Literature also reached its apogee with Nguyễn Du, Nguyễn Đình Chiểu, Bà Huyện Thanh Quan and Nguyễn Công Trứ, while historical and geographical studies received careful treatment. The so-called Huế blues are world-famous for their delicate and delightful porcelain design and enamel. Handicrafts were given official support and each village had its own speciality, thus the village of Thổ-hà was well known for its baked clay ceramics.

With the assumption of power by Gia-long, Vietnam entered into that period of her history which saw the beginning of effective Western influences in the form of technical ideas and administrative services as well as the introduction of Western religious and political ideologies. Gia-long's successors, however, were less sympathetic to these new trends and their attitudes often showed themselves in severe repressions and persecutions against those who responded to Western ideas and to the Christian missionaries in particular. Their hostility jointly with French colonial aspirations resulted in French military intervention and eventual conquest of Vietnam. In

1863, the French annexed South Vietnam and in 1874, they invaded North and Central Vietnam. Within ten years they had consolidated their authority over the whole country. From then until World War II, Vietnam was a part of French Indochina. However, during the whole French occupation, the drive of the Vietnamese people for independence was frequently manifested in various forms. Such are, for instance, the uprising of the Phan Đình Phùng at Hà-tĩnh from 1893 to 1895, the foundation of the nationalist movement Đông-kinh nghĩa-thục by Prince Cư'ờng Để, Phan Bội Châu, and Phan Châu Trinh in 1906, the revolutionary movement under the leadership of Nguyễn Thái Học in 1931, etc. . . .

Following the fall of the French in 1940, the Vichy regime assented to the occupation of French Indochina by the Japanese, an occupation which went on until 1945. After the Japanese defeat in August 1945, the Vietminh forces created the Democratic Republic of Vietnam and prevailed upon Emperor Bảo-đại to abdicate his throne. The French authorities who had returned in Vietnam in early 1946 gained control over most of the population centres but found their authority challenged by communist regime in the north. There followed six months of indecisive negotiations. During this period, French troops were permitted to land in the north. But by December 1946, it became clear that no agreement could be reached and on December 19 the Vietminh forces attacked the French on a wide front. The war lasted for eight years and ended in July 1954 with the Geneva Conference which, against her people's will and agreement, divided Vietnam at the 17th parallel into two parts: the North Vietnam under communist control and the South remaining the State of Vietnam with Bảo-đại as Chief of the State. Later on, in October 1955, the Republic was proclaimed by a referendum in South Vietnam[1].

CHAPTER II

VIETNAMESE CULTURE AND CHINESE CULTURE

In the light of the above-outlined geographical and historical background of Vietnamese culture, we can trace the various exogenous cultures which have, in the past, contributed to the Vietnamese cultural heritage. Chronologically, we have discerned the successive influences of the following cultures. In the first millenium B.C., there had been the Austro-Asiatic culture. Next there came the Indian culture, from the second century B.C. to the middle of the sixth century A.D., the Chinese culture, from the second century B.C. to the nineteenth century A.D. and finally, Western culture, from the nineteenth century up to now. Of all these cultures, it was the Chinese culture which has exerted the most long-lived influence on Vietnamese culture and so, will it be the first to hold our attention.

1. SOCIAL STRUCTURE AND POLITICAL INSTITUTIONS

Before it was invaded by the Chinese General Chao T'o in 207 B.C., Vietnam, which was successively called

Văn Lang and Âu Lạc, had been only a feudal state with a strict and well-defined hierarchical and decentralized system. The supreme authority was a king under whom there were such other lords as Lac-hầu or marquises and other civilian officers and Lạc-tu'ó'ng or military officers. The area occupied by these lords was called Lạc-điền and given them by the king as their own fiefs. The functions of the king, Lạc-hầu and Lạc-tu'ó'ng were hereditary. The male children of the king were entitled Quan-lang, his female children, Mệ-nàng or Mỵ-nu'o'ng. This social structure of ancient Vietnam, vestiges of which have been found in Dongsonian culture, lasted until the year 43 A.D. when the Chinese General Ma Yüan vanquished the two Tru'ng sisters and brought Giao-chỉ back under the Chinese yoke. From then on, it was the adoption of Chinese institutions by the Vietnamese and the virtual obliteration of their own ones. Thus, the social structure of ancient Vietnam was, more or less, patterned after that of ancient China, especially in the triple view point of the family system, the village system and the government system.

The family system was the root of the society both in ancient China and in ancient Vietnam. Here and there, it was based on the Confucian doctrine of social status. Its major principle was what Confucius called *Ming-fen*. *Ming* means name and *fen* means duty. A name, as explained Lin Yü-tang, is a title that gives a man his definite status in any society and defines his relationships with others. Without a name, or a definition of the social relationship, a man would not know his *fen* or duties in that relationship and hence would not know how to behave. The Confucian idea is that if every man knows his place and acts in accordance with his position, social order will be ensured[2]. This Confucian principle of *Ming-fen* also accounts for the status of the Vietnamese family members. At the top of each family, the pater-familias or gia-tru'ở'ng exercised an absolute authority over his wife and children. He had full power to act and command. He was invested with rights prevailing over those of the other members of the family. He was alone qualified to manage their estates and incomes which had to become a common property. His wife, far from being his equal, was his inferior, which is explained by the status assigned to the Vietnamese woman both in the family and in the society. Everywhere the Vietnamese woman has been pushed to the background. At home, she was inferior to her husband and in the social life, she could not take part in public affairs. She had more duties than rights and in such a family of the Confucian type as the old Vietnamese family, her most important duty was to bring her husband a male child to perpetuate his family.

Many such families just summarized above, if coming from a common ancestor, formed a clan called họ or tộc which consisted of many branches or chi. The tộc-tru'ở'ng or the head of clan was the head of the oldest branch. A clan had a temple of ancestors which was to be erected in the house of the tộc-tru'ở'ng, who was at the same time entrusted with keeping the gia-phả or the genealogy of the clan. He was also responsible for the cult of ancestors. He had the usufruct of a part of the clan's patrimony for the service of ancestral cult. All members of the clan gathered at his house to perform the worship ceremony on the anniversary of the death of each ancestor as well as on many feast days in the year. By this cult of ancestors was materialized the Confucian duty of filial piety, a bond which tied the living with the dead.

A Vietnamese village was constituted by a group of patriarchal families whose members shared the same family name. The family was, therefore, the fundamental cell of the old Vietnamese society. According to Prof. Nguyễn Đăng Thục, it is most likely that, at the beginning, a number of families united together for protection against incursions of pirates and to clear and cultivate the marshlands of the delta; relationship was based on their economic activities. As their collective life developed, these spontaneous groups thus had to get organized administratively with a view to receiving from the central authorities their consecration as an autonomous social cell. Later on, after the establishment of the monarchy and its mandarin system which were patterned after those of China, the state never ceased to promote the establishment of communes for the colonization of the country and its expansion towards the south of the Indochinese Peninsula[3]. As the village system is nothing but the family system raised to a higher exponent, some characteristics of the Vietnamese family were found again in the Vietnamese village. Firstly, just as each family was headed by the paterfamilias, so was each village by the head or the chairman of the Council of Notables. Secondly, in a Vietnamese village there was a system of a hierarchy of social classes which also proves to derive from the above-mentioned Confucian principle of *Ming-fen*. Each village could draw up this system as it found it suitable. However, two principal practices were the most common, namely the vu'o'ng-tu'ó'c or the practice of *human right* and the thiên-tu'ó'c or the practice of *divine right*. The former conferred the communal power on those who took their office from the king, while the latter gave the power to old people. Thirdly, just as each family had its altar dedicated to the cult of ancestors, each village had a temple for the worship of a tutelar god. Finally, let us mention the feeling of attachment for one's own village, which bounds together the people of the same village. This feeling is called in Chinese t'ung-hsiang kuan-nien.

The government system in ancient Vietnam was that of Chinese-type monarchy, i.e. that of absolute monarchy by divine right. In accordance with this system, the king was the Son of Heaven. He represented the celestial sovereign to govern the people, and he alone was qualified to render account of his terrestrial mandate to Him. Men and gods, all were submitted to his authority. Like the paterfamilias towards his own children, he also had an absolute power over his own people. He was "the father and mother" of his subjects. Property and life of everyone belonged to him. As the head both of the kingdom and of his own family, he had the double duty to celebrate the cult of imperial ancestors and to offer up to the celestial sovereign the sacrifice called nam-giao. Under the leadership of the king, there was a vast body of officials or mandarins divided into two orders: the civil and the military. The sovereign had at his disposal two ways of recruiting civil and military officials: the hereditary way and the way of literary and military competitions, both inspired after Chinese practices. Under the administrative control of the officials, there was the huge mass of the population. In principle, there were no true social classes, all subjects being ranked below the king as those who were invested with his authority. However, there were always, after the Chinese pattern, preferred social categories with scholars (sĩ) ranking first, followed by farmers (nông), artisans (công) and merchants (thu'o'ng).

According to Đại-Việt sủ'-ký ngoại-kỷ toàn-thu':

"In the spring of the year 939, Ngô Quyền proclaimed himself king, set up a body of officials, established court protocol and designed uniforms for the army and administration."[4)]

All these institutions were inspired and patterned after Chinese institutions. When Đinh Bộ Lĩnh opened the

Đinh dynasty in 968, he went on the same lines by building royal palaces, improving court protocol and regularizing military and civilian statutes. Moreover, by giving his reign the name of Thái Bình, he was the first Vietnamese king to adopt the Chinese practice of naming the year of a king's reign. With regard to monetary system, he was also the first Vietnamese king to manufacture two coins both patterned after the Chinese coins and bearing the inscriptions of Thái Bình Hu'ng Bảo and Thái Bình Thông Bảo respectively. The next dynasty, the early Lê also borrowed such Chinese institutions as the system of fallow fields regulation and the local administrative system of lộ (province), phủ (prefecture) and châu (sub-prefecture). From the Lý to the Nguyễn, all national dynasties of Vietnam, without any exception, more or less patterned their political institutions after the Chinese ones. Under the Lý, the first imperial college was founded in 1076, where the best scholars were sent to teach Chinese classics. In 1089, a hierarchy in the mandarin system was established. Top-ranking officials were chosen to hold the offices of Thái-su', Thái-phó, Thái-úy, Thiếu-su', Thiếu-phó and Thiếu-úy. The remainder of the hierarchy was divided into civilian and military positions. As to the army, its reorganization was based on T'ang and Sung patterns. In the field of criminal law, a penal code was for the first time compiled from Chinese documentation by order of King Lý Thái-tôn.

Under the Trần, upon the instructions of King Trần

Thái-tôn, two digests of laws and regulations were compiled referring to the practice of the previous Chinese and Vietnamese dynasties in the matters concerned. Entitled Quốc-triều thông-chế and Quốc-triều thư'ó'ng-lễ respectively, the former comprised twenty volumes and the latter ten volumes. Later on, King Trần Hiến-tôn ordered Tru'o'ng Hán Siêu to compose a digest under the title of Hoàng-triều đại-điển as well as a penal code to be promulgated. With regard to the status of court officials, it was the same as under the Lý dynasty. In 1242, King Trần Thái-tôn divided the kingdom of An Nam into twelve lộ. Each lộ had its own census book and was under the control of An-phủ-sú' (governor in charge of peoples' welfare), who was assisted by two deputies. Then came the Đại tu'-xã and the Tiểu tu'-xã; each administered from two to four villages, while a xã itself was directly headed by a Chánh-sú'-giám. In the field of education, the first examination for the selection of Thái-học-sinh or the doctorate degree was held in 1232. Three categories were defined in a classification system called Tam-giáp. The classification became more elaborate in 1247 with the Tam-khôi which divided the first category into three separate classes: Trạng-nguyên (first prize winner in the competitive examination at the king's court), Bảng-nhãn (second prize winner) and Thám-hoa (third prize winner). Examinations in the field of three religions–Confucianism, Buddhism and Taoism–called Tam-giáo (Three Religions) were established at the same time and were held throughout the kingdom.

After having freed the national territory from the rule of the Ming, Lê Lọ'i came to the throne in 1428 under the royal title of Lê Thái-tồ. As soon as he came to power, he set on reorganizing the kingdom. The new administrative unit was subdivided into phủ (prefecture) and huyện (sub-prefecture). Smaller units were constituted by xã (hamlet). He also reorganized the judicial system and the penal code taking for model that of the Chinese dynasty of T'ang. Under the reign of Lê Thánh-tôn, the kingdom was administratively divided into twelve đạo, each with three authorities: the military, Đô tồng-binh, the administrative, Thù'a-chính, and the judiciary, Hiến-sát. The Giám-sát ngự'-sủ' (Imperial Inspectors) supervised the affairs of the đạo. Later on, after the annexation of Quảng-nam province from Champa, the country was divided into thirteen xú' (region), which, in their turn, were subdivided into 52 phủ, 172 huyện and 50 châu. Smaller units within the phủ and the huyện were hu'o'ng, ph'ò'ng, xã, thôn, trang, sách, đồng, nguyên and tru'ỏ'ng totalling 8,006 units. In the educational field, the examination procedures were reorganized and patterned after the Ming system.

The Nguyễn, the last national dynasty in Vietnam, showed yet more clearly the Chinese influence. With regard to political and administrative reforms, we should mention the creation of six Bộ (Ministries) by Emperor Gia-long: Bộ-lại (Ministry of Public Offices), Bộ-hộ (Ministry of Finances), Bộ-lễ (Ministry of Rites), Bộ-binh (Ministry of National Defense), Bộ-hình (Ministry of

Justice) and Bộ-công (Ministry of Public Works). All of these ministries were headed by a Thu'ọ'ng-thu' (Minister) and supervised by a Đô-sát-viện(Council of Censors), which also played the role of advisors to the Emperor. On the regional level, the national territory was divided into 23 trấn and 4 doanh. The trấn was further subdivided into phủ, huyện and châu. With reference to legislation, Emperor Gia-long, in 1811, charged Nguyễn Văn Thành with the compilation of a new code called the Gia-long Code which was a blend of the Lê's code and the Chinese code of the Ch'ing dynasty. Finally, under the Nguyễn dynasty, the Chinese institution of Co'-mật-viện (Top Secret Council) was adopted by Emperor Minh-mạng in 1834[5].

2. CONFUCIANISM, BUDDHISM AND TAOISM IN VIETNAM

According to Jean Herbert, metaphysical, religious, spiritual and mystical preoccupations with all the ritualism which goes with them, are the principal foundation of the Asian traditional life of which they impregnate all the domains, from the familial and social life to sciences and arts[6]. Thus, religious systems and ethical concepts, far from being separated from each other, have been always confounded together, especially in China and in Vietnam. In other terms in these countries religious faith has been a way of life, a way essential to man for the realization of his destiny in the society and the universe. Consequently, such religious systems as Confucianism, Buddhism and Taoism, borrowed in the past by the Vietnamese from China, have been at the same time ethical concepts for them.

Confucianism is considered to have been introduced into Vietnam as early as the first century A.D. Two Chinese governors of that time, Hsi Kuang and Jên Yen were the most instrumental in its introduction. Hsi Kuang was governor of Giao-chỉ from 1 to 25 A.D. As he followed the example of General Governor Têng Jang (Đặng Nhu'ọ'ng) and did not recognize Wang Mang's usurpation of Han dynasty, many officials and scholars faithful to the dynasty came to take refuge in Giao-chỉ. During their stay in the country, they fruitfully helped Hsi Kuang to spread the Chinese culture there by founding Chinese schools to teach the Vietnamese farming technique and Confucian ethics. As for Jên Yen, he came to govern Củ'u-chân district in about 29. He is said to have taught the use of farming implements and the rites of marriage. However, despite these important contributions of Hsi Kuang and Jên Yen, it was not until the second period of Chinese domination that more advanced studies of Confucianism could be registered. According to the annals, before the year 189, students of Giao-chỉ had obtained the degree of Hsiao-lien and Mao-ts'ai in literary competitions in China. Under the reign of the Chinese Emperor Ling Ti (168–169), one of those students named Lý Tiến was appointed governor of Giao-chỉ and later on two others, Lý Cầm and Tru'o'ng Trọng were nominated to the posts in Chinese administration[7].

At the end of the late Han dynasty, Shih Hsieh came to Giao-chỉ as governor. After giving Giao-chỉ the new name of Giao-châu, he did his best to develop the teaching of Chinese characters and Confucianism. His achievements earned him the title of Sĩ Vu'o'ng or the King of the Scholars. Later on, under the T'ang domination (618–907), Chinese studies and Confucianism reached a far higher degree of their development. But, what seems to be rather a paradox, it was after Giao-châu had gained its independence from China that Chinese characters and Confucianism enjoyed more general popularity in the country. Their growing role in Vietnam was materialized in many cultural institutions successively set up by the national dynasties, especially in the field of education.

Lý Thánh-tôn's reign (1054–72) was marked by the king's order to cast statues of Confucius, Chou Kung[8)] and the seventy-two sages to be worshipped in a temple called Văn-miếu. Under Lý Nhân-tôn's reign (1072–1127), a literary competition consisting of subjects on three religions was held in 1075 for the recruitment of mandarins. The first laureate of this contest, Lê Văn Thịnh was appointed Thái-su' (King's Counsellor) and the others were appointed teachers at the Imperial College which was opened in 1076. A new competition was organized in 1088 to select the members for the newly-founded Academy. The first successful laureate of this competition was Mạc Hiền Tích on whom was conferred the title of Hàn-lâm thị-độc (Academy High Chancellor). Finally, in 1089, the hierarchy of mandarins was set up. Also patterned after the Chinese one, it was divided into nine classes of two grades each, and the mandarin's rank depended upon the degree of success reached by them in the literary competitions organized for selecting public officials. All these innovations of the Lý testified to the development of education and consequently of Confucianism on a wider scale for everyone instead of exclusively for the upper or privileged class of society.

Under the Trần, simultaneously with the continuing encouragement of Buddhism expansion, new Confucian-inspired institutions were promoted for educational purpose. As the Lý had initiated the three-subject literary competition for the recruitment of government officials, the Trần improved it in 1232 by organizing a competition at a higher level called Thái-học-sinh for the doctor's degree and ranked the successful candidates doctors of first, second or third class according to their merits. Other changes were brought about by the kings of Trần in literary competitions. In the three religions competition of the year 1247, the degrees of licentiate and bachelor of letters were created below the doctorate. In 1253, another imperial college, the Quốc-học-viện (Institute for National Studies) was founded to teach the four classics, as well as the five canonical books of Confucianism. Under Trần Thánh-tôn's reign (1258–78), the educational system developed even further. The king opened a school for the training of scholars and put it under the management of his younger brother, Trần Ích Tắc. However, during the last years of the Trần dynasty, the development of education was not achieved as it had been scheduled owing to the massive invasions of the Mongols. People then came to prefer feats of arms rather than success in literary competitions. But despite such a critical situation, many warriors and scholars such as Trần Hu'ng-đạo, Phạm Ngũ Lão, Đặng Dung and Trần Quang Khải proved to be writers of great value. Their works showed the high degree of development reached by the study of Confucianism at the end of the Trần dynasty.

During the Ming occupation, Confucianism of Sung school was imposed in Vietnam by the Chinese authorities. Under the Lê dynasty, studies and teaching of Confucius' doctrine attained to their apogee. Soon after his victory over the Ming and the recovering of national independence, King Lê Thái-tổ set about renovating old institutions and reorganizing the system of education. Apart from the Imperial College frequented by the children of government officials, new schools were established in the capital and even in such smaller administrative units as phủ and huyện to teach the doctrine of Confucius. Examinations were organized throughout the country to give all learned men the opportunity to make themselves known to the royal court and to be appointed to various posts. Under Lê Thái-tôn (1434–42), some minor changes were made in the examination procedures. At the same time it became customary to proclaim aloud the names of successful candidates and to celebrate their glorious return to their native villages. Under Lê Thánh-tôn more improvements were initiated. The king personally presided over the competition held in the capital. Suitable measures were taken to avoid fraud and select really able men for the body of mandarins and officials. Candidates coming from other localities than the capital could enjoy hostel accommodations in a school located behind the Temple of Confucius.

During the Trịnh-Nguyễn internecine war classical textbooks still continued to be imported from China into the north of the country. But in 1734 Trịnh Giang forbade their importation in view of building up the national economy. Examinations such as the thi-hu'o'ng or regional examinations were held every three years. In the south, the Nguyễn also organized examinations to select able public servants who, once appointed by the royal court, were classified into three categories according to their functions: administrative affairs, tax questions or rites and ceremonies. Despite such brilliant achievements by the Trịnh and the Nguyễn or later, by the Tây-so'n under Emperor Quang-trung's reign, Confucian studies and Confucian-inspired education began to decline after the Lê dynasty. It was not until the reign of Emperor Gia-long of the Nguyễn dynasty that they could see a rapid recovery. Confucianism was again revived and developed. Temples were built in honour of Confucius. Scholars of the previous dynasty of Lê were then appreciated and appointed Đốc-học or supervisors and promoters of education in the provinces. Confucianism received a new impulse under Emperor Minh-mạng.

In 1822, literary competitions were organized to choose the Tấn-sĩ or doctors. The examinations which had been held every six years were now to be held every three years. Although the changes he brought to the various literary competitions proved to be successful for the recruitment of qualified civil servants, the emperor soon realized the shortcomings of the educational system of his time. He said:

"For long, our examinations have been leading our students to a useless goal. No literature can be fully developed when it is bound by too old and strict rules. If this is the way by which our people are being educated, then really talented men will become scarce!"[9)]

However, he did not succeed in finding a suitable system to replace the one he criticized and the same Confucian-patterned education remained basically unchanged under the successive reigns of the Nguyễn dynasty.

Next to Confucianism, Buddhism was introduced from China into Vietnam. However, there is evidence that it was brought to the country on the one hand by the Chinese refugees in North Vietnam after the death of Emperor Ling Ti in 189, and on the other by Buddhist pilgrims of Indian, Indo-Scythian and Sogdian extraction from the third to the sixth century. Later on, the Chinese monks who went on pilgrimage to their Holy Land always took the road of Giao-châu, which was then the only convenient way from Canton to the Indian coast, and there is good reason to suppose that these travellers had contributed to the spreading of Buddhism in the country. In any case, according to I Ching, a Chinese pilgrim in the seventh century, many Chinese bonzes had stayed for a certain period of time in North Vietnam on their way to India. Such monks as Vận-kỳ, Mokṣadeva and Khuy-sung who, at that time, went on pilgrimage to Buddha's homeland were natives of Giao-châu[10]. From then on, Buddhism never stopped developing in Vietnam. As early as the end of the Chinese domination, under the reign of King Đinh Tiên-hoàng (968–79), Buddhist communities were founded and Buddhist temples and pagodas were built. Especially, Buddhism was the most favoured under the dynasties of the Lý and the Trần. Several kings themselves took the cassock or retired into a pagoda after their abdication. Under King Lý Thái-tôn's reign, numerous pagodas were built and bonzes were sent to China in search of sacred texts. Under the Trần, King Trần Anh-tôn ordered in 1297 the publication of the Buddhist texts brought back from China by a royal delegation.

From the fifteenth century to the sixteenth century, owing to the prodigious development of Confucian culture introduced into Vietnam by the Ming, Buddhism received less favour from the kings. However, many Buddhist sects which had been established in the country did not cease to flourish. The first of them was found by Vinītaruci, a Brahmin, native of south India. As early as his youth, he had travelled in western India for studying Buddhism. After following the patriarch Sêng-ts'an in China, he came to Vietnam where he settled in Pháp-vân pagoda in Hà-đông province. There, he founded a new Buddhist sect which never stopped prospering since the seventh century. The second Buddhist sect was founded by Wu-yen-t'ung (Vô-ngôn-thông), a native of Kuang-chou, who came and settled in Kiến-so' pagoda in the village of Phù-dổng in Bắc-ninh province, where he died in 828. The third sect was created in the middle of the eleventh century by a Chinese known under the name of Ts'ao-t'ang (Thảo-đu'ò'ng). It developed in the very court of King Lý Thánh-tôn who was considered one of the first successors of the founder. In the thirteenth century another sect called Trúc-lâm (Bamboo-wood) was founded on Mount Yên-tủ' in Quảng-yên province by the three patriarchs under the Trần, namely King Trần Nhân-tôn, Pháp-loa and Huyền-quang; the first one being just the grandson of King Trần Thái-tôn, the author of a doctrinal book entitled Khóa-hu' lục (*Path of Dhyāna's Emptiness*). About at the end of the sixteenth century, the Chinese bonze Shui-yüeh (Thủy-nguyệt) introduced in North Vietnam the Chinese sect of Ts'ao-tung, which he transmitted to his Vietnamese disciple Tôn-diễn, who died in 1709.

In 1676, a new sect was founded under the name of Liên-tôn (Lotus sect) by a prince of Trịnh. This prince was a disciple of a Chinese bonze named Cho-kung (Chuyết-công), a native of Fukien who came to North

Vietnam from the south then under the rule of the Nguyễn after travelling through Cambodia. One of the greatest success achieved by this bonze was the conversion of Queen Diệu-viên, wife of Lê Thần-tôn and her daughter Diệu-tuệ who were both of the Trịnh family. In the same period, the prince of the Nguyễn family who ruled over the Southern Court also helped to develop Buddhism again. Pagodas were built all over his territory and the first one called Thiên-mụ dates from 1601. It was erected in the west of Huế by Prince Nguyễn Hoàng. The successors of this prince were also fervent adepts in Buddhism. They built many pagodas in Central Vietnam and offered asylum to the Chinese bonzes who fled from China because of the Manchu invasion.

Taoism, simultaneously with Confucianism, had been introduced into Vietnam before Buddhism at the beginning of the first Chinese domination. Originally, it derived from the philosophical doctrine of Lao-tzu centring on the metaphysical notion of man's oneness with the universe. Until the end of the Trần dynasty, it was generally appreciated by the Vietnamese people as much as Buddhism and Confucianism. Under Trần Thái-tôn's reign, for instance, it was officially admitted as a subject for the examinations and, later on, under the Mạc dynasty (1527–1592) and then in the course of the Trịnh-Nguyễn internecine war, it inspired most of the poets and writers of both the Northern and Southern Courts. However, from the end of the Trần dynasty,

Taoism began to degenerate into a kind of polytheism with innumerable gods the supreme one of which is Ngọc-hoàng (Emperor of Jade). Under the sovereign rule of Ngọc-hoàng there are, besides a large number of deities, Diêm-vu'o'ng (King of the Hell), Long-vu'o'ng (King of the Waters) and the household gods, one of which is the Táo-quân (God of the Kitchen). Taoism, in its degenerate form as summarized above, has left in Vietnam many superstitious practices and religious cults. The former ones include sorcery, witchcraft, horoscopy, chiromancy and geomancy, all of which are also derived from Chinese Taoism. Among the religious cults originating from Taoism, there are, for instance, the cult of Chu'-vị or spirits of the three worlds (the sky, the earth and the water) and the Nội-đạo or cult of heroes and heroines. The cult of Chu'-vị consists in the worship of the numerous deities in the sky, on earth and in the water. If a deity is masculine, he is called Đú'c-ông (our lord). A feminine one is called Thánh-mẫu (our saint mother). Often a deity is young and is called Cậu (young master) and Cô (young mistress). The mortals can communicate with them only through a medium in the form of a man called Ông-đồng or a woman called Bà-đồng.

In some of Vietnamese temples national heroes and heroines are worshipped. For instance, General Trần Hu'ng-đạo of the Trần dynasty who won many victories over the Mongols and succeeded in recovering national independence was worshipped as a national hero in the temple built for his cult in the village of Vạn-kiếp in Hải-du'o'ng province. This hero is also believed to be the divine killer of evil spirits. Another temple was erected near Hanoi for the cult of two heroines, Tru'ng Trắc and Tru'ng Nhị who headed an uprising against the Chinese oppressors in 39 A.D. The third temple built in the nineteenth century in Gia-định province was dedicated to Marshal Lê Văn Duyệt. On the eve of every new year many people go to this temple to have their future foretold by diviners and to pray for good luck (*pl. 13*).

3. LANGUAGE, WRITING AND LITERATURE

Although the Vietnamese language is likely more linked with the Austro-Asiatic family, its lexicon includes a great number of words borrowed from many other languages among which the Chinese language has been the most important supplier. In the course of over one thousand years of Chinese domination, the Vietnamese people had adopted and used the Chinese writing system which was called Chũ'-nho or scholars' script. From about the ninth century and long after the country was freed from the Chinese rule, Chinese characters continued to be employed in government transactions as well as in education, correspondence and literature. Under such circumstances, a large quantity of Chinese words were introduced into Vietnamese language. Chinese loan-words which were imported along a double process, the scholarly one and the vulgar one, consisted of two categories of words: the classical Sino-Vietnamese and the vulgar Sino-Vietnamese. The former category included loanwords coming from Chinese characters which remained the same but received a Vietnamese pronunciation. According to Henri Maspero, such loanwords dates back approximately to the end of the T'ang dynasty and showed many similarities with the Chinese dialect of the then capital, Chang-an, from which they were, to some extent, very likely to derive[11]. We quite share this point of view and also recognize that a quantity of Sino-Vietnamese words took shape in the tenth and eleventh centuries, created as they were by the Confucian scholars on the basis of T'ang and Sung dictionaries of rhymes. However, we should also take into account so many other Sino-Vietnamese words which did not cease to be introduced into Vietnamese language from the tenth century to now. Therefore, it often happens that one Chinese character has two ways of pronunciation, one as classical and the other as vulgar Sino-Vietnamese. For instance, the Chinese characters 萬 and 晚 meaning *ten thousand* and *late* respectively, have given vạn and vãn in the classical Sino-Vietnamese and muôn and muộn in the vulgar Sino-Vietnamese.

Very long before the romanized system of writing was officially adopted, the Vietnamese people had used the Chinese writing system which was called Chữ-nho (*pl. 1*). Later on, however, when they felt the need to write in their own language which the Chinese script was not able to express, they started borrowing Chinese characters of which they made various combinations to represent ideas and concepts and also to phoneticize native sounds. Hence was invented the Chũ'-nôm or demotic system for writing which looks somewhat like Chinese characters but may be undecipherable to the Chinese themselves. Although dating back at least to the fourteenth century, and proving to be in most cases both semantic and phonetic, this writing was used only for popular literature and non-official documents. This humble rank of the Chũ'-nôm was perhaps due to the fact that in traditional Vietnam Chinese was held in high esteem and carried with it all the prestige of an educational medium with the sanction of civil service examinations from the village level to the national level at the Court of Huế (*pl. 2*).

After recovering their independence from the Chinese in the tenth century, the Vietnamese people, by lack of a national script, went on using Chinese characters as their educational and literary medium. Therefore, if we put aside the vast body of the people's literature orally transmitted from the remotest times up to now, the oldest form of Vietnamese literature was the Vietnamese literature in Chinese characters, which had been prior to that in demotic script and in romanized script.

The first three national dynasties have left only two short poems written by two Buddhist monks Đỗ-thuận and Ngô-chân-lu'u in honour of Li Chiao (Lý Giác), a Chinese envoy, before his return to China. Under the Lý dynasty, several poetical works were composed either by Buddhist monks or by high-ranking court officials, who were deeply imbued with Buddhist thinking. Bonze Khánh-hỷ was the author of Ngộ-đạo thi-tập (*Collected Poems on the Way*) and Bonze Bảo-giác was the author of Viên-thông-tập (*Collected Poems of Viên-Thông*). Such other bonzes as Không-lộ and Từ'-đạo-hạnh also left poems nearly all of which developed various themes of Dhyāna. Among the non-religious writers, let us especially mention General Lý Thu'ờ'ng Kiệt who was famous for the following poem he composed in 1076, when the country was threatened by the Sung invasion:

Nam quốc so'n hà Nam Đế cu'	南國山河南帝居
Tiệt nhiên định phận tại Thiên-Thu'	截然定分在天書
Nhu' hà nghịch lỗ lai xâm phạm	如何逆虜來侵犯
Nhũ' đẳng hành khan thủ bại hu'.	汝等行看取敗虛

"The Southern Kingdom with its Mountains and rivers belongs rightly to the Southern King.
The Book of the Heavens has so willed.
Then, why did your hordes invade our territory?
Very soon, you will see, your forces will be annihilated."12)

Under the Trần dynasty, many kings and members of the Buddhist clergy went on to compose poetry, together with such famous Confucian scholars as Mạc Đĩnh Chi, Tru'o'ng Hán Siêu and Chu Văn An. But the most valuable documents of this dynasty consisted of historical writings, the most important of which was the Đại-Việt sử'-ký (*Historical Memoirs of the Great Viet*) of thirty volumes composed by Lê Văn Hu'u under the reign of King Trần Thái-tôn. Many other books covering various subjects such as laws, rites, poetry, military and science were also produced during this era. Unfortunately, a great amount of them were seized and sent by the Ming army to China. The best-known of these lost books were the Hình-thu' (*Penal Code*) by King Lý Thái-tôn, the Hình-luật (*Penal Law*) by King Trần Thái-tôn, the Quốc-triều thu'ờ'ng-lễ (*Court Ceremony of the Kingdom*) by the same king, the Tú'-thu' thuyết-u'ớ'c (*Summary of the Four Books*) by Chu Văn An, the Binh-thu' yếu-lu'ợ'c (*Treatise on Strategy*) by General Trần Quốc Tuấn, the Thi-tập (*Collected Poems*) of Nguyễn Trung Ngạn, the Nam-Việt thế-chí (*Historical Memoirs of Nam-Viet's Dynasties*) and the Việt-sử' cu'o'ng-mục (*Annals of Viet's History*) by Hồ Tôn Thốc.

After a short eclipse, the Vietnamese literature in Chinese characters flourished again before attaining to its apogee with such masterpieces as the Bình Ngô đại cáo (*The Proclamation on the Pacification against the Chinese*) by Nguyễn Trãi, the Thiên-nam du'-hạ-tập (*Spare Times in the South of the Sky*) and the Quỳnh-uyển củ'u-ca (*Nine Songs of the Imperial Garden*) by King Lê Thánh-tôn and his Academy of Letters, the Chinh-phụ-ngâm (*Complaints of the Warrior's Wife*) by Đặng Trần Côn, the Lĩnh-Nam Trích-Quài (*Super-*

human Beings of Linh-nam) composed by Lý Tế Xuyên and revised by Vũ Quỳnh, the Truyền-kỳ mạn-lục (*Vast Collection of Legends*) by Nguyễn Dũ', the Tục Truyền-kỳ (*New Collection of Legends*) by Đoàn Thị Điểm, the Lủ'-trung tạp-thuyết (*A Traveller's Notebook*) by Bùi Huy Bích. With regard to historical writings composed under the Lê, let us mention such valuable works as the Đại-Việt sử'-ký toàn-thư' (*A Complete History of the Great Viet*) by Ngô Sĩ Liên, the Việt-giám thông-khảo (*A Thorough Historical Study of Viet*) by Vũ Quỳnh.

An outstanding place must be reserved for Lê Quý Đôn (1726–84), whose works constitute a precious mine of information on Vietnam's history and her traditional institutions. This encyclopaedist writer has left many masterpieces, very remarkable for their scholarship and their variety. Let us mention, among others, Đại-Việt thông-sử' (*A Complete History of the Great Viet*), the Phủ-biên tạp-lục (*Miscellanea on Marches' Administration*), the Bắc-sú' thông-lục (*Notebook on a Mission in the Northern Country*), the Quế-đu'ờ'ng thi-tập (*Collected Poems of Que-duong*), the Toàn-Việt thi-lục (*A Complete Collection of Vietnamese Poetical Works*), the Quần-thu' khảo-biện (*Commentary on Various Works*), the Vân-đài loại-ngữ' (*Essays on Various Subjects*), the Danh-thần-lục (*Biographies of the Most Famous Mandarins*) etc....

Chinese script literature remained prosperous from the nineteenth century until the beginning of the twentieth century. With regard to the Nguyễn dynasty, especially, many masterpieces of poetry and historical writings worthy to be mentioned are the Phu'o'ng-đình thi-văn-tập (*Collected Poems of Phuong-dinh*) by Nguyễn Siêu, the Cao-chu-thần thi-tập (*Collected Poems of Cao-chu-than*) by Cao Bá Quát, the Thảo-đu'ờ'ng thi-tập (*Collected Poems of Thao-duong*) by Phạm Quý Thích, the Bắc-hành thi-tập (*Collected Poems on an Ambassadorial Tour in China*) by Nguyễn Du, the Khâm-định Việt-sử' thông-giám cu'o'ng-mục (*Authorized History of Vietnam*) compiled under the reign of Emperor Tự'-đú'c, and the Lịch-triều hiến-chu'o'ng loại-chí (*Institutional History of National Dynasties*) by Phan Huy Chú.

As far back as the thirteenth century, while Chinese characters were officially employed in literature and government transactions, Vietnamese scholars had felt the need to devise such a script as would be able to transcribe native sounds. Hence the Chũ'-nôm or demotic script was invented. The first writer to have used this new writing system was Nguyen Thuyên in the thirteenth century and many writers such as Nguyễn Sĩ Cố and Chu Văn An were said to have followed his example. But the literature in Chũ'-nôm knew effectively full bloom from the sixteenth to the nineteenth century, when Chinese patterns still prevailed in poetry and in prose. Vietnamese writers who very soon struggled out of the Chinese models began to work in other directions: the narrative verse and the plaintive ballad. Đoàn Thị Diềm was the author of the very popular ballad Chinh-phụ-ngâm (*Warrior's Wife Ballad*). Equally famous is Cungoán ngâm-khúc (*Complaint of a Palace Maid*) by Nguyễn Gia Thiều (1741–98). As for the narratives (truyện nôm), we will have to mention Hoa-tiên (*The Flowered Letter*), Kim Vân Kiều (*Story of Kim, Van and Kieu*), Phan-trần, Nhị-độ-mai, Lục-vân-tiên, Thạch-sanh and Nũ'-tú tài.

All these ballads and narratives together with most works of Vietnamese literature in Chũ'-nôm were to be transcribed into romanized script from the nineteenth century after Quốc-ngũ' was officially adopted all over the country.

4. ARCHITECTURE, SCULPTURE, MUSIC AND THEATRE

Except for Loa-thành, the City of Shell built in 255 B.C. by King An Du'o'ng Vu'o'ng of the Thục dynasty, almost nothing was left of prehistoric Vietnam's art. The first era in the history of Vietnamese arts, which has been called the Đại-la era and lasted from the ninth to the eleventh century A.D., has already shown a strong Chinese influence conjunctly with the Indian influence (*pl. 5a*). But as early as the thirteenth century, some specific features began to emerge in Vietnamese arts, which proved to be eminently original in the Lê era, before undergoing again the Chinese influence in the Nguyễn era. The Chinese influence which was being exerted on Vietnamese arts from the ninth century down to the nineteenth century can be traced through such aspects as architecture, sculpture, painting, music and theatre.

The Chinese influence on Vietnamese architecture is clearly revealed in many Chinese-patterned buildings, in their decorative designs and in the choice of their site. Like most of Asian countries' architecture, the Vietnamese was imbued with religious spirit. That is why religious monuments always took the first rank of all. Buddhism, Taoism and Confucianism have through centuries inspired Vietnamese architecture. These three Chinese systems of religion have respectively presided over the setting up of Chùa or Buddhist temple (*pl. 10*), the Đền or Taoist temple, and the Văn-miếu or the temple of Confucius. They have also inspired the various decorative designs of religious monuments as well as civil buildings. Scenes from the Hell's torments and from Taoist mythology can be seen in Buddhist and Taoist temples. As for Confucianist-patterned designs, they are ornamentally used for house buildings.

The Chinese influence was also visible in the choice of the site for the buildings whatever they might be. In this matter, the geomancer played an important role. In the old times and even nowadays especially in the countryside, he was of necessity consulted, whenever a religious temple, a dwelling house or a tomb had to be built, so as to locate the best site for it. The choice of the site was considered most important, because, according to the popular belief, the happiness and the life of all the family members depend upon it.

The Chinese influence, far from limiting itself to the religious monuments, was also felt in the structure of the imperial palaces, of the mandarins' abodes and of the buildings for military purposes. The imperial palaces and the mandarins' abodes, generally patterned after their Chinese equivalents, were characterized by their shape which frequently was similar to that of the Chinese characters 工 (kung : work) and 門 (mên : gate) and by their roof suggesting the image of a dragon or a phoenix (*pl. 7*). Among the Chinese-patterned constructions for military purposes, let us mention the citadel of Đại-la built by the Chinese General Kao P'ien in 867, and the citadel of Tây-đô built in Thanh-hóa by the throne-usurper Hồ Quý Ly at the end of the fourteenth century.

Sculpture played an important role in old Viet-nam. Like Vietnamese architecture, it also centred on the religious field and showed many foreign influences among which the Chinese one was the most prominent. Chinese inspiration was particularly obvious in such ornamental motifs as bats, squirrels, fabulous animals like dragons, unicorns, phoenixes, cranes, symbolic plants and flowers like bamboo, plum-tree, and chry-santhemum. It was also revealed through some kinds of sculptures in stone, such as gravestones and stelae. Old Vietnamese gravestones bore carved Chinese charac-ters indicating the names, titles, dates of birth and death of the deceased persons. They were usually erected on the back of a stone giant-turtle as the symbol of quiet and continuous life in the other world. Many of these old gravestones still exist in the imperial tombs in Huế and in several religious temples throughout the country. As far as stelae are concerned, the most characteristic ones with regard to the Chinese influence were those erected to commemorate the people's gratitude towards famous great men in the past or to record some important events of the national history. Such are, for instance, stone stelae which can be found today in the temples dedicated to General Trần Hu'ng-đạo and the Tru'ng sisters, and in the Temple of Confucius in Hanoi to commemorate the literary competitions that successively took place there from 1442 to 1779. Finally, let us mention the biggest Chinese-patterned bronze statue in old Vietnam, the statue of the God Trần Vũ worshipped in Quan-thánh Temple of Hanoi.

Besides such pictures as found on carved, inlaid and embroidered works, painting in old Vietnam consisted merely of a few works depicting religious scenes such as the pictures of Thập-điện (Temple of ten great Buddhist deities), of Bạch-hổ (white tiger) and of Ngũ-hổ (five tigers)[13]. Like Vietnamese architects and sculptors in the past, Vietnamese painters themselves used to take their inspiration from Chinese models and borrowed from them such motifs as the Tú'-linh (four sacred animals: dragon, unicorn, tortoise and phoenix), the Tú'-quí (four seasons: spring, summer, autumn and winter), the Ngũ-phúc (five blessings: riches, honours, long-life, health, and peace), the Tam-đa (three abundances: happiness, riches and long-life). As for painting practices, water-coloured paintings on silk or rice-paper or on wood cuts were adopted.

Vietnamese music in the past underwent the double influence of Chinese music and Indian music. Under the Chinese domination Chinese music must have been rather familiar to the Vietnamese people. However, no written proofs can yet be found to ascertain the influence of Chinese music during that period. According to Dr. Trần Văn Khê, three successive eras can be distinguished in the history of Vietnamese music: the first period from the tenth to the fifteenth century, the second period from the fifteenth to the eighteenth century and the third period from the nineteenth century to the eve of World War II[14]. In the course of the first era, the Indian influence through Cham music competed with the Chinese one and sometimes predominated over the latter. According to Lê Tắc, a Vietnamese historian in the fourteenth century, there were under the Trần dynasty two orchestras: the bigger one or Đại-nhạc and the smaller one or Tiểu-nhạc[15]. The Đại-nhạc was reserved for the sovereigns and high dignitaries and made use of Cham instruments. While the Tiểu-nhạc was at the disposal of the other social strata and included Chinese instruments. Moreover, under the Lý and the Trần dynasties, the influence of Chinese music was merely limited to the field of the dramatic music, perhaps owing to the introduction, at that time, of Chinese theatre into Vietnam. During the second era, from the Hồ dynasty to the Lê dynasty, Indian influence yielded precedence to the Chinese one and Vietnamese music began to take model after Chinese music. At the beginning of the Lê dynasty, under the reign of King Lê Thái-tôn, a new ritual music was set up by Lu'ò'ng Đang who took off the music of the Ming period. From then on, the Vietnamese adopted Chinese instruments and Chinese styles. The royal court set the fashion which began to be felt in the whole national music.

Chinese influence on Vietnamese music under the Lê dynasty was officially recognized by King Lê Thánh-tôn who, in 1470, ordered Trần Nhân Trung, Đỗ Nhuận and Lu'o'ng Thế Vinh to undertake research on Chinese music. Two organizations in charge with music were established: Đông-văn and Nhã-nhạc. The former was charged with score-composition and the latter with singer-training. Both of them were placed under the control of a court dignitary called Thái-thu'ò'ng. However, they were on their decline, since 1578, when the Giáo-phu'ò'ng or popular orchestra began to supersede. In the beginning of the nineteenth century, new regulations were framed for the ritual music. The Giáo-phu'ò'ng which had previously operated on the occasion of official ceremonies gave way to such other orchestras as the Nhã-nhạc or the regal music, the Đại-nhạc or the grand music, the Tế-nhạc or the small music, the Dao-nghinh-nhạc or the reception music, the Nũ'-nhạc or women's orchestra, the Ty-chung or group of bells and the Ty-khánh or group of lithophones. Civil music as well as military music was all patterned after Chinese music. The

Chinese influence on Vietnamese music lasted on until the latter came in touch with Western music in the twentieth century to give birth to the modernized music (*pl. 9*).

With regard to Vietnamese theatre, chronologically, there have been the Hát-bộ or the traditional theatre, which was introduced into Vietnam in the thirteenth century, the Hát-chèo or popular theatre which dates back to the fourteenth century, the Hát-cải-lu'o'ng or renovated theatre which came into existence in South Vietnam in the course of World War I, and the Kịch or westernized theatre initiated by Nguyễn Văn Vĩnh's translations from Molière's comedies in 1921 and 1935. Of these four kinds of theatre, the first one will exclusively retain our attention now, because of its Chinese origin and inspiration. According to Vietnamese annals, the Trần who defeated the Yüan caught a prisoner Li Yüan-ki, a distinguished Hát-bộ actor, who taught the Vietnamese Chinese theatre songs and dances. The performance of a Chinese play called Si-wang-mu was presented by Li Yüan-ki to the royal court and was greatly appreciated[16]. Thus, Chinese theatre was introduced into Vietnam by a Chinese actor at the end of the thirteenth century and was adopted by the Vietnamese under the name of Hát-bộ (gestured theatre) or Tuồng-Tàu (Chinese theatre).

The Hát-bộ was primarily performed in the royal palaces and was reserved only for the sovereigns and the royal court dignitaries. It was favoured under such dynasties as the Trần and the Lê, but during the Trịnh-Nguyễn wars, it was only appreciated by the lords of Nguyễn in the Southern Court. However, it was not until the beginning of the nineteenth century that the first theatre for the Hát-bộ was set up by Emperor Gia-long in the very precincts of the Imperial Palace in Huê̂. Most of the successors of Emperor Gia-long took interest in the traditional theatre. Under the reign of Emperor Minh-mạng (1820–40) the official troupe was headed, as dancing and singing master, by a Chinese actor named Kang Koung-heou. Emperor Tụ'-đú'c (1847–83) invited men of letters to cooperate with him for composing new plays. Emperor Thành-thái (1889–1909) who went in enthusiastically for theatrical art, sometimes willingly played himself the part of an actor. With respect to the troupes of Hát-bộ for the public, they only made their appearance at the beginning of the nineteenth century. Many performances were given by them in the remotest villages through the century until on the eve of World War II when the traditional theatre was superseded by the Hát-cải-lu'o'ng or the renovated theatre. The Hát-bộ which is now more than seven centuries old, shows such main similarities with Chinese theatre as related to the plays' subjects, stage arrangements, stage properties, actors' costumes, making-up and playing technique as well as parts distribution.

Emphasis has been laid only on the most characteristic

fields where Vietnamese culture has been influenced by Chinese culture. Nevertheless, such is not the exhaustive extent of the Chinese influence, which, as a matter of fact, has covered many other aspects of Vietnamese life and civilization. However, despite the vast and powerful ascendancy of Chinese culture in the past, Vietnam has been able to shape an eminently national culture with such other exogenous ones as Indian culture, Austro-Asiatic culture and Western culture.

CHAPTER III

VIETNAMESE CULTURE AND INDIAN CULTURE

The efforts of cultural anthropologists have usually been directed at stressing too much the influences of Chinese culture, thus sometimes overlooking the influences of Indian culture. The influences of Indian culture should be examined in three aspects, namely, its direct influences on Vietnam, its indirect influences through Chinese culture and those through Cham culture.

Central and South Vietnam had received an earlier acculturation from India than North Vietnam. This is due to the fact that this area had been formerly the sites of such Hinduized states as Champa, Funan and Chen-la. As for North Vietnam, it began to be open to Indian culture only during the years from the second century to the sixth century, through the expansion of Indian Buddhism which, prior to Chinese Buddhism, was brought into North Vietnam by way of sea-route. Moreover, during the whole period of Chinese domination, a great number of monks from Sogdiana, from the Indo-Scythian Empire as well as from India continued to come to the country to preach Buddhism. Scriptures from

Vietnamese monks in the thirteenth and fourteenth century also referred to this fact as follows:

"Under the Han dynasty, many Buddhist monks from the north came to our country both by sea and land to preach their religion, such as Mārajīvaka, K'ang-sêng Hui and Mou-po."[17)]

The Chinese history of the Wu also recorded that:

"Shih Hsieh was a powerful governor in Chiao-chou (Giao-châu) respected by the local population. In his comings and goings, bells and high-sounding stones could be heard. His imposing escort moved forwards to the sound of cornets and flutes. Roads were filled with vehicles, by the side of which were marching groups of *Hu* barbarians, burning incense. There were usually several tens of them."[18)]

According to Sylvain Lévi, *Hu* in Chinese language of the third century meant "inhabitants of the West," i.e. of Central Asia or of India[19)]. So the so-called *Hu* barbarians might be Indian who came to Vietnam by sea-route. The Biography of Vietnamese Monk Thông-biệm also quoted a passage from the biography of Monk T'an-t'ien who reportedly said to King Kao-tsu of Sui dynasty as follows:

"The people of Chiao-chou can communicate with India more easily than ourselves, though Buddhism has already entered into China, but not yet reached our Chiang-tung. The inhabitants of Chiao-chou have already built twenty stupas and they have more than five hundred religious people who recited fifteen series of scriptures. That is why it is said that Chiao-chou is more advanced in Buddhism than China. Several monks had come over there to preach Buddhism at that time, such as Mārajīvaka, K'ang-sêng Hui, Kalyāṇaruci and Mou-po.... Your Majesty's desire is to send some monks of ours to preach Buddhism over there, but I do not think they are needing anyone."[20]

The Buddhist book Pháp-vũ thụ'c-lục also tells us that in the third century a Brahmin named Kandra came to Giao-châu at the same time with Mārajīvaka from eastern India[21]. These records reveal that there had been direct intercourses between India and Vietnam by way of sea-route and that consequently Buddhism was introduced into Vietnam by Indian Buddhist monks. Thus, from the end of the second century to 544 and also under the early Lý dynasty (544–548), Buddhism in the country was only at its beginning, although a certain number of monasteries had been built. Vietnam at that time was undergoing the direct influence of India rather than that of China in the Buddhism area, so that except a few Indian scholars who had been devoted to the translation of Buddhist scriptures, nobody had considered getting Chinese Buddhist scriptures from China. From 603 to 939, when the influence of Chinese Buddhism gradually transcended that of the Indian, there were still some monks coming from India to preach Buddhism. For instance, in 580, Vinītaruci came to Vietnam, took up residence at Pháp-vân pagoda and founded the Buddhist sect of Dhyāna. Thus Indian Buddhism had directly influenced Vietnamese culture before it was superseded by Chinese Buddhism. Another direct influence of Indian culture can be traced through a few Vietnamese words which, according to Souvignet, seem to have been derived from Sanskrit. Let us quote below the most probable ones among them[22].

Skt, *hīna* (vile, abject) Vietnamese, hèn.
Skt, *rūpa* (shape, look physionomy) Vietnamese, dâp.
Skt, *śuci* (clean) Vietnamese, sạch sẽ.
Skt, *dvi, dva* (some, two) Vietnamese, vài.
Skt, *buddha* (he who knows, Buddha) Vietnamese, Biêt, Bụt.
Skt, *pūrṇa* (having hunger satisfied) Vietnamese, no.
Tamil, *beut, bet* (steadfast, motionless, very quiet) Vietnamese, bặt bặt.

As far as its indirect influences are concerned, we should distinguish between two categories: Indian influences through the channel of Chinese culture and Indian influences through the channel of Cham culture. As for Indian influences through the channel of Chinese culture, much has been said about the Buddhism (see pp. 28–31). Here they should be traced in such fields as sculpture, music and language.

Vestiges of Vietnamese culture unearthed by Louis

Bezacier who considers them as representative specimens of what he calls Đại-la art, include carved stone works from Phật-tích in Bắc-ninh province, material from Hanoi in the vicinity of the race course, terra cotta figures from Phật-tích, also a stele and brickwork from Long-đội-so'n in Hà-nam province. The gritstone sculpture from Phật-tích, according to his conjectures, probably belongs to a stupa erected for celebrating the victory of the Chinese General Kao P'ien over Nan Chao in 866 to 870. Including a Lokapāla, a Vajrapāṇi and a Kinnarī, this stupa makes up what he calls the Phật-tích style, whose Indian characteristics are clearly revealed by the presence of small flowers arranged in bandeau as ornament for the hair on all the Kinnarī's heads, by the presence of the same kind of flowers with which the Vajrapāṇi's tunic, the Lokapāla's gown, the Kinnarī's torso as well as the carved dancers' and musicians' dress are strewn, and finally by the presence of little naked manikins between the foliated scrolls of the Long-đội-so'n friezes and the Phật-tích console. The same Indian elements can be found again, but already modified by Chinese influences, in vestiges from the brick-built stupa erected in 1057 by Lý Thánh-tôn on the very site of Đại-la citadel. These vestiges whose characteristics are terra cotta decorative motifs based upon flowers, elongated dragons and foliated scroll patterns together with cabochons have been classified by Louis Bezacier among art works of the Lý dynasty's style[23].

Vietnamese music itself has been influenced by Indian

music. Till the end of the dynasties of Northern and Southern China, several musical instruments were introduced into China from India, passing through Central Asia. Emperor Yang Ti of the Sui dynasty collected all the instruments and divided them into nine groups among which were some instruments from Khotan and India. The hu-ch'in, a stringed musical instrument used by the ancients, came from India during the Han dynasty and became very popular. The p'i-p'a, another important musical instrument of the guitar-type used during the Han and the T'ang dynasties came from Egypt through Arabia and India. Most of those instruments were used both by Chinese and Vietnamese people.

Finally, let us say a word about Indian influences on Vietnamese culture through the channel of Chinese Buddhism in the field of language. We know that the Indian Buddhists who came to China to preach their faith contributed certain tables which were helpful in spelling of words. Shên Kung, a Buddhist priest, is said to be the author of the system, and the dictionary Yü-p'ien (*Discrimination of Language*) was one of the first extensive works in which it was employed. There was also a famous historian Shên Yo to whom the discovery of the four tones has been attributed. This Chinese system of four tones shows many relationships to the tones of Vietnamese words, especially those of Sino-Vietnamese words. We can also mention the enrichment of words from Sanskrit through Chinese translation. As we know, during the eight hundred years between the Han and the T'ang dynasties, prominent Chinese Buddhist scholars created more than 35,000 new phrases and words by two methods. On one hand, they combined two Chinese words to evolve a new meaning, such as chên-ju. *Chên* (chân in Sino-Vietnamese) means *real,* ju (nhu' in Sino-Vietnamese) means likely; their combination means Bhūtatathatā. The word is fundamental to Mahāyāna Buddhism, implying the absolute, the ultimate source and character of all phenomena. On the other, they adopted a Sanskrit word with its original sound; for instance, San-mei coming from Samādhi and Na-mo coming from Namo. Most of these words have been integrated into Vietnamese language[24].

Indian influences through the channel of Cham culture have affected many aspects of Vietnamese life and culture. Let us mention here the most important ones like religious beliefs, fine arts and folkloric literature.

As a Hinduized state, Champa welcomed from India both Buddhism and Brahminism. According to Vietnamese annals, many Buddhist monks of Chinese origin as well as of Cham origin came from Champa to North Vietnam, where they preached Buddhism or founded new Buddhist sect. Among them are, for instance, Haha Mara, the Cham monk who in the tenth century took up his residence in a pagoda of North Vietnam, and a Chinese monk Ts'ao-t'ang who came from Champa under the reign of King Lý Thánh-tôn and founded a new sect of Dhyāna in Vietnam. Brahminism, which probably was introduced into Champa at the same time as Buddhism, has left many marks in Central Vietnam from the Annam Gate to Phan-thiết province. With regard to Islamism, it was brought into Champa only in the tenth or eleventh century. Here let us only give the terms Hồi Hồi and Ngu'ờ'i Hò'i which were used by the Vietnamese in reference to Islamism and the Chams. In the field of religious beliefs, mention must also be made of the worship of snakes, fishes, trees, stones and of evil spirits, which can be found in old India, Champa and Vietnam.

Cham arts, although very typical of the Cham people's spirit, had been deeply influenced by Indian culture. From the seventh century to the end of the fifteenth century, they developed through various stages. All through these stages, Cham arts have left several vestiges which can still be found in Central Vietnam in the form of such art works as brick-built towers, animal reliefs, Cham deities sculptures and stone pillars of worship along the roads (*pls. 5b, 6*). Moreover, some elements of Cham sculpture were re-employed by the Vietnamese, who occupied the kingdom of Champa. Let us mention, for instance, great doorkeepers and beasts like the stone elephants which perhaps were used by Cham artists to line the access road to a temple, and more particularly, the Ông-phỗng or Cham stone statuettes of kneeling manikins which can still be found now in some Vietnamese temples dedicated to great men of national history.

Indian influence on Vietnamese music and songs

through Cham influence probably dates back to the eleventh century. In 1044, King Lý Thái-tôn personally led an expedition against the kingdom of Champa which had neglected during the first fifteen years of his reign to keep up its duty of allegiance toward Vietnamese court. Jaya Simhavarman II, King of Champa, lined up his troops south of the river Ngũ-bồ. But finally they incurred heavy losses with five thousand men taken prisoners and thirty elephants captured. Cham General Quách Gia Gi, at the end of his resources, killed his king and brought his head to the Lý as a sign of submission. Lý Thái-tôn then proceeded to Vijaya, capital of Champa (now in Hu'o'ng-thủy prefecture, Thù'a-thiên province), levelled its citadel and captured Mỵ Ê, the favourite of Cham king and all of the maids of honour. According to Khâm-định Việt-sử', these people knew how to play the tune called Khúc Tây-thiên (western sky tune) which was a part of their dances and songs' repertoire[25]. In 1202, by orders of King Lý Cao-tôn, the Royal Academy of Music composed a new tune called Chiêm-thành âm (Champa's tune) which was characterized by its specifically languorous rhythms. Such are the historical circumstances of the introduction of Điệu-nam or southern songs into Vietnam. As far as musical instruments are concerned, some of them, despite their Sino-Vietnamese names, may be considered to have come from India through the channel of Champa. Among them are the wooden castanets called phách, the transverse flute called ống-sáo and the drum called phạn-cổ, a forerunner of today's trống-co'm which seems to derive from the Ḍamaru of ancient India (*pl. 8*).

One of the most popular forms of Vietnamese folkloric literature consists of the vast body of the anonymous tales and legends which from time immemorial have been transmitted orally throughout the country. Many of these tales and legends can be easily connected with their Chinese sources. However, some of them have been more likely of Indian origin and probably date back to the time when Buddhism was introduced into Vietnam from India through the channel of Champa. They must have been patterned after such Indian popular epic poems as the Bhagavadgītā, the Mahābhārata and especially the Rāmāyaṇa which was wide-spread in Champa. But we should also take into account, as another source of inspiration, Indian fables which are to be found in various Indian books. Besides numerous detached apologues, which they are very fond of alluding to in their everyday conversations, the Indians have regular collection of old and popular fables called Pañca-tantra (the five tricks). With respect especially to Vietnam's relationship with Champa in the field of folkloric literature, let us take into account, among the most pertinent indications, the existence of many Cham and Vietnamese folktales which seem to have proceeded from the same Indian sources. For the enjoyment of our readers, we hope it would not be superfluous to quote in an Appendix two excerpts from *The Stork and the Shrimp* by Đỗ Vạng Lý with our best anticipated thanks to the author.

CHAPTER IV

VIETNAMESE CULTURE AND INDONESIAN OR AUSTRO-ASIATIC CULTURE

Among all the exogenous cultural substrata which have ever contributed to the making of Vietnamese culture, the most subjacent, the most momentous, too, has been the Indonesian or Austro-Asiatic one. Most of its elements, more or less modified by its inter-reaction with subsequent cultural patterns, can yet be recognized in many aspects of Vietnamese culture: in the fields of linguistics, mythology and ethnology.

The Vietnamese language has been enriched by innumerable Chinese words and expressions. However, it is not admitted by Orientalists as having originated from the Chinese language. German linguists like Kuhn and Himly were inclined to believe that the Vietnamese language belongs to the Peguan, T'ai or Mon-Khmer group[26]. Henri Maspero maintained that it is of T'ai origin[27], and Souvignet traced it to the Indo-Malay family[28]. A.G. Haudricourt has recently refuted the thesis of H. Maspero and concluded that the Vietnamese language must be properly placed in the Austro-Asiatic family between the Palaung-wa group in the northwest and the Mon-Khmer group in the southwest[29]. None of these theories fully explains the origin of the Vietnamese language. One fact, however, remains certain: Vietnamese is no more a pure language. It seems to be a blend of several languages, ancient and modern, encountered through history following contacts between foreign peoples and the Vietnamese people.

Consequently, the Vietnamese language was enriched with new words from each successive wave of immigrants among whom were the Indonesians. For these considerations with regard to the origin of the Vietnamese language we share Prof. Nguyễn Đình Hòa's following opinion:

"For the time being, inclusion in the broad Austro-Asiatic family, which comprises a number of languages widely scattered through southeastern Asia and generally surrounded by languages of other families, can be considered adequate, until the results of lexico-statistics or glotto-chronology bring us more definitive conclusion."[30]

One of mythic themes which were the most widely spread over all the Austro-Asiatic-stocked peoples concerns the origin of ethnic races. In many Southeast Asian and particularly Indochinese countries there is a whole cycle of legends related to this theme. "Among the Palaungs (a Mon-Khmer people), for instance, the story is told of a serpent maiden who fell in love with the son of the solar king and loved him, and eventually was delivered of three eggs. Due to a misunderstanding with her lover, who had been called back home by his father, the Naga princess took two of the eggs and threw them into the Irrawaddy River. One of the eggs moved upstream to Man Maw (Bhamo), where it was taken out of the river by a gardener and his wife and put in a golden casket as a curiosity. A male child hatched out of the egg and the gardener and his wife brought him up under the name of Hseng Nya, and afterward of Udibwa (Born of an egg). Later married to the daughter of a Shan chief, he became the father of two sons, one of whom became emperor of China, while the other became the ancestor of all the chiefs of the Palaungs. The second egg also drifted down the Irrawaddy until it was picked up by a washerman and his wife. From this also came a male child, who grew up to be the king of Pagan."

The same mythic theme can be found again in a folktale from Hsen-Wi, one of the northern Shan states of Burma. According to this, "there was an old couple who lived on the bank of Lake Nawng Put, and they had a son, who fell in love with a Naga, a princess who came out of the lake one day in human form and talked with him. The princess also loved the lad, and took him to the country of the Nagas, where she explained matters to her father, the King of the Dragons. The father then allowed all the dragons to assume human form, so that his son-in-law might feel at home. The princess and her husband lived happily together, until the annual water festival of the Nagas came round. During this festival, the Nagas assumed their dragon shape and disported themselves in the lakes of the country. The princess, however, told her husband to stay home during the festival but, overwhelmed with curiosity, he climbed up the roof of the palace and was very much dismayed to find the whole of the country and the lakes round about filled with gigantic writhing dragons. In the evening all the dragons returned to the palace in human shapes. Likewise the princess; but, when she came to her husband, she found him dejected and wanting to go back to his own father and mother. The princess accordingly accompanied him back to his own country, but told him that she could not stay there. On her departure, she told him that she would be delivered of an egg from which a child would be hatched, and that she was to feed the child with the milk which would ooze from his little finger whenever he thought of her. Then she said that if either he or the child were ever in danger of difficulty, he would strike the ground three times with his hand, and she would come to his aid. She laid the egg, plunged into the lake, and returned to the country of the Nagas. The child was born in due course and grew up under the care of the boy's parents into a splendid youth. Later he married a beautiful princess, inherited a kingdom and had a long and prosperous reign of seventy-two years."[31)]

This theme of the marriage between human beings and

aquatic animals was also the foundation of our national myth, related to Lạc Long-quân and Âu Co'.

According to popular tradition, some more than four thousand years ago, King Đế Minh, a descendant of the Chinese King Thần Nông (Shên Nung) went on a tour to the south and met at Ngũ-Lĩnh (Wu-ling) mountain (Hunan province) a fairy whom he married. She bore him a son who was given the name of Lộc Tục. Lộc Tục received from his father the southern part of his kingdom named Xích Quỷ, and reigned under the royal title of Kinh Du'o'ng Vu'o'ng. One day, Kinh Du'o'ng Vu'o'ng called on the God of the Seas and married his daughter, Long Nũ'. From this union was born a son named Sùng Lãm. Sùng Lãm succeeded to his father under the royal title of Lạc Long-quân. Later on, he withdrew to his former palace of the sea. But, as the Xích Quỷ kingdom was invaded by the army of Đế Lai, a Chinese Emperor, her inhabitants invoked Lạc Long-quân who came back from his palace under the sea and saved the country from Đế Lai's oppressions. Lạc Long-quân then married Âu Co', the daughter of Đế Lai. Âu Co' bore a pouch of one hundred eggs which gave one hundred male children. Lạc Long-quân and Âu Co' shared the sons between themselves. Half of them went with their father to the South China Sea, the other half accompanied their mother to the mountains located in the area of Phong-châu. Once in Phong-châu (now Bạch-hạc, North Vietnam), the fifty sons who had followed Âu Co' named their eldest brother the first king to reign over the new kingdom. He was Hùng Vu'o'ng, and this kingdom was called Văn Lang.

Thus, we can see that the national myth of the Vietnamese people shows the same elements as its congeners in most of the Southeast Asian countries, one of those elements being the maritime character of the folktales[32)].

A more careful investigation of ethnological affinities between the Austro-Asiatic peoples and the Vietnamese people would take a whole volume. In this short study, we may therefore limit ourselves to the wearing apparel and ornaments, the types of dwelling, and the family organization of Vietnam in early times.

The most persistent thing about Vietnamese dress is yet the cái-khô̂ (loincloth) for men and the cái-váy (petticoat) for women. The cái-khô̂ consisting of one piece of cloth was wrapped once and a bit around the waist and intermediate space of the hips. It is still used as an undergarment by women, as an outer garment by fishermen and mountaineers of the highlands. As for Vietnamese women, especially country women of North Vietnam and of the northern part of Thanh-hóa province, they wear a kind of skirt like the Indonesian one. Both men and women wear jacket and petticoat with diminutive sleeves like Indonesian people. Also like Indonesian people, Vietnamese people wear a turban made of a piece of cloth wrapped around their head. As mentioned in An-nan chih-yüan by Kao Hsiung-chêng, a Chinese historian of the Ming dynasty, Vietnamese males wore a loincloth while females wore a petticoat during the tenth century[33]. As we can read in Đại-Việt sủ-ky by Ngô Sĩ Liên, the fishermen of ancient Vietnam up to the Trần dynasty used to tattoo themselves in the guise of a dragon before going into the sea in order to protect themselves from the attacks of sea creatures[34]. Besides these, there are still other vestiges of Austro-Asiatic customs such as the custom of blackening the teeth and the use of the betel nut.

Also in the field of architecture, while remaining eminently original, Vietnamese architecture shows many affinities with Austro-Asiatic architecture. According to Lu'o'ng Dú'c Thiệp[35], the characteristics of Vietnamese architecture lie in its reflection of the living mode of the Vietnamese people, who lived in the delta. Being not very fortunate and having not enough vital space, they are reduced to build their dwellings from the materials they can find around. Since wood and bamboo are the building materials most commonly available, all edifices are essentially a system of columns and rafters on which rests the roof strengthening the whole with its weight. One of the many characteristics of Vietnamese architecture is precisely the role of the columns which serve as support for the roof. On the other hand, the tropical climate explains why there are few walls or partitions separating the interior apartments and it explains the frequent absence of a door. One sees the entrance wide open or perhaps shaded with a blind. The most ancient type of shelter consists of four roofs, two main and two accessory roofs leaning on a wooden frame system which is in turn supported by a system of columns. Concerning Vietnamese and Indonesian roof-structure, we think further studies should be undertaken for a better understanding of the religious meaning which may lie in the various crossing ways of rafters. In any case, the Vietnamese Đình is certainly a parallel of such houses on piles as can still be found in Indonesia today.

The family organization in traditional Vietnam has been under the overwhelming influence of Confucian concepts which give precedence to men. That is why, as early as the beginning of Chinese domination, Vietnamese society has been a patrilineal one, where the woman was subordinate to her father before her marriage, to her husband after her marriage, and to her sons after her husband's death. This status of women in ancient Vietnam was based upon a Confucian precept called Tam-tòng (three subordinations of women). However, one can suppose that in the remotest times, before undergoing Chinese influence, the Vietnamese family may have been a matrilineal one. According to Lu'o'ng Dú'c Thiệp[36)], the uprisings of Tru'ng sisters in 40 to 43, and of Lady Triệu Ẩu against Chinese yoke in 248 testify to the existence of matrilineal family system in ancient Vietnam. As a matter of fact, the Vietnamese woman, in spite of the humble status reserved for her by official legislation which has been of Chinese inspiration, has always proved to be better treated in practice. Other proofs of this matrilineal system can be found in the biography of Đinh Bộ Lĩnh, founder king of the Đinh dynasty, and Lý Thái-tổ, the first king of the Lý dynasty. Neither of them knew whose son he was[37]. In other respects, women have always been the main force behind in an agricultural country like Vietnam.

In this connection, the two following Vietnamese proverbial sayings are the most significant.

"Chồng cầy, vợ' cấy, con trâu đi bừ'a" : "The husband is ploughing, the wife transplanting the rice seedling while the buffalo is harrowing."

"Lệnh ông không bà'ng cồng bà" : "The man's orders are not worth the woman's jobs."

Recently, Prof. Robert Lingat has contributed many important findings about the matrimonial system of joint estate. According to him, contrary to official legislation, the respective marriage portions of man and woman have been put into community[38]. Thus, the Vietnamese woman has, at least in practice, never been in the status of subjection, which bears testimony to the strong survival of Indian influence and of Austro-Asiatic influence in Vietnamese social life. Those are a few ethnological data we can take into account within the very narrow scope of this book. Let us, however, mention such other important research matters on the Austro-Asiatic and Vietnamese ethnological affinities as related, for instance, to seasonal festivals, and those in the fields of naval ethnography as well as of physical and spiritual culture of the Vietnamese people.

CHAPTER V

VIETNAMESE CULTURE AND WESTERN CULTURE

1. HISTORICAL OUTLINE

Though there are several evidences to show that the contact between Vietnam and the West began as early as the second century B.C., regular contacts between Western countries and Vietnam started when the Portuguese came to Southeast Asia and took Malacca in 1511. After the taking of Malacca, Portuguese envoys repaired to the royal court of Siam. Thence, Christian missionaries penetrated into Indochina. As early as 1550, they set about preaching the Catholic faith to the Cambodians. The first apostles were the Portuguese Dominicans of Malacca, and then the Spaniards of Manila. One of them, Diego Aduarte landed at Hội-an (Faifo) to evangelize the Cochinchinese from 1593 to 1596. North Vietnam attracted the Jesuits who remained there for more than 150 years. Giuliano Baldinoti, an Italian, went there in 1626 and Alexandre de Rhodes in the following year.

During the sixteenth and seventeenth centuries, Vietnam was in the midst of the Trịnh-Nguyễn internecine war. The Europeans, therefore, had two different partners to contact in Vietnam. In South Vietnam, which was ruled by the Nguyễn, Hội-an was the key port where the trade was carried out by Chinese and Japanese as well as other peoples from abroad. The Portuguese opened there a trade centre in 1637, but unfavoured by the Nguyễn, they had to leave in 1641. The Dutch came next to the Portuguese, but were not very heartily welcomed for they also sought relations with the north. In 1641, as they killed a native servant suspected of theft, a naval action from the Nguyễn ensued, in which they were put to rout. Things improved again in 1651 and the Dutch established at Thuận-quảng a trade centre which they maintained for three years before leaving.

In 1613, an English merchant coming from Japan presented the Nguyễn with precious gifts, as a precursory step to trade negotiations but he happened to be killed by the villagers. In 1695, another English merchant arrived in Hội-an and succeeded in reaching a trade agreement but, did not return for its implementation. In 1777, Charles Chapman was sent by the English East India Company on a commercial mission to the South Vietnam which, from Quảng-nam southward, was then occupied by the Tây-so'n. In 1664, a Frenchman named Véret was sent by the French Company of India to study trade possibilities on Pulo Condore Island. In the same year, another Frenchman, Pierre Poivre arrived at Đà-nẵng, then proceeded to Phú-xuân where he was received by the lord of Nguyễn.

While the Portuguese were taking a peculiar interest

in developing trade in South Vietnam, the Dutch were allowed to open a store in 1637 in Phố-hiến in Hu'ng-yên province, which soon became an important business centre. But as they refused to give their assistance against the Nguyễn, they were dismissed from the Trịnh's favour and by 1700 they had left Phố-hiến. In 1672, the English were allowed to settle in Phố-hiến, but, as business grew worse, they also left in 1694. In 1680, Chappelain was sent to the north by the French Company of India. He was authorized to settle in Phố-hiến.

In 1682, the French ship St. Joseph brought gifts from Louis XIV to the lord of Trịnh who returned the courtesy himself. The French continued to come to Phố-hiến but did not engaged in any commerce there, and from the early eighteenth century on, they paid more attention to the Nguyễn in the south.

"Economically, in spite of the establishment of a few trade centres in Vietnam, the impact had been almost insignificant for many reasons until the end of the eighteenth century. Firstly, the foreign traders did not stay in the country for a long time, and they made little attempt to expand their trade activities on a wider scale and on a permanent basis, mainly because of the political instability which characterized Vietnam at that time. Secondly, all business transactions were performed with the governmental authorities and not with private local merchants. Finally, luxury items and weapons formed the most part of the imports from the West, neither of which contributed to the welfare of the masses."

While the traders were engaged in their business, Catholic missionaries came to Vietnam. The first one was Ignatio who, as early as 1533, had come to preach in Nam-định province. In 1550 Gaspard de Santa Cruz landed in Hà-tiên which was still a province of Cambodia. In 1585, two Dominicans, George de la Motte and Louis Fonseca evangelized in lower Cochinchina. In 1596 Diego Aduarte preached in the Nguyễn's territory. In the first half of the seventeenth century, the Jesuits came to Vietnam. Early in 1615, two of them, an Italian named Francesco Busomi and a Portuguese named Diego Carvalho arrived in Tourane. They founded in Hội-an Cochinchina's mission which, in the beginning, included for the most part Portuguese and Italian Jesuits. Encouraged by the first success, the Jesuits set up to extend the preaching to the north. In 1625, Giuliano Baldinotti was sent there. His report was instrumental in setting up a Jesuit mission for North Vietnam. In 1626, Alexandre de Rhodes, who had been in the south since 1623, was chosen to head this mission. The French Jesuit stayed in the north from 1626 to 1630 when he was expelled by the Trịnh. In the south the Nguyễn themselves prosecuted Catholic preaching. Alexandre de Rhodes then fled to Macao but continued to come back to South Vietnam until he was definitively expelled from there. In 1645, he was sent back to Europe by his superiors to ask for more assistance, missionaries and bishops.

By that time, since 1641, the Dutch, who were Protestant, became masters of Malacca and took away from the Portuguese the control of the roads to Japan and China. Prior to this event, the Papacy, foreseeing Portugal's loss of privilege in Asia, planned to preach Christianity out of her patronage. The Congregation of Propaganda founded as early as 1622 set to work on the evangelization of Asia. In 1636, they appointed to the East Indies an apostolic vicar depending directly on them and working free from any interference of the Portuguese authorities. It was in this context that Alexandre de Rhodes arrived in Rome in 1649, where he submitted to the Congregation a plan for the establishment in Vietnam of an episcopate independent from Portuguese patronage. The task of organizing a local clergy was entrusted to bishops who were to be appointed not directly from Rome but in the areas where they preached to non-Christian people. Negotiations with the Portuguese took a long time, during which the Congregation of Propaganda began to publish such first works of Alexandre de Rhodes as the narrative of his voyages, a catechism both in Latin and Vietnamese in 1650 and Vietnamese-Portuguese-Latin dictionary in 1651 (*pl. 3*)[39].

In the meantime, Alexandre de Rhodes, unable to restrain his impatience, went back to Paris where he did his best to speed up the sending of more priests for the Catholic missions in Vietnam. He succeeded in winning the sympathy and support both of the French church and the French aristocracy who agreed to help him and appeal to Rome. But he was unexpectedly sent on mission to Persia where he died in Ispahan in 1660. However, the French aristocracy continued to collect money to support the episcopates in Vietnam. Then in 1658 two French apostolic vicars, François Pallu and Lambert de la Motte were appointed by Rome to Vietnam's episcopates.

By that time, the policy was prevailing in France which aimed at developing together religious, political and commercial activities for the glory of the French king. Under these circumstances, the Holy Sacrament Company planned to found the Company of China for the Propagation of Faith and the Establishment of Commerce[40)]. François Pallu took a boat for his travel to Vietnam. But his boat was destroyed by a typhoon and the Company's plan was cancelled. Later in 1664 the *Société des Missions Etrangères* was founded and Colbert also set up a new company for trade in the East Indies. Pallu embarked again for Vietnam but his boat was struck anew by a typhoon on the coast of the Philippines. He had then in hand a plan for the establishment of a company in North Vietnam. Thus, up to the end of the eighteenth century, French trade was represented in Vietnam only by missionaries.

At the same time, Christianity also developed rapidly in the country. But Vietnamese authorities were anxious about its increasing spread and began to take proscription measures. In 1662, Trịnh Tạc issued his instructions for moral amendment in which the cardinal virtues of Confucianism were taken as basic principles to be observed by all Vietnamese subjects who were bound to evince loyalty towards their lords and devotion to their country. All books teaching Buddhism, Taoism, and Christianity were prohibited. Stronger measures were taken in 1665 for the proscription of the Christians. In Hội-an the Christians were sentenced to death. About the middle of the seventeenth century, preaching of Christianity was banned both in the north and the south.

Despite the proscription, Catholic missions continued to work for the evangelization of Vietnam either openly or clandestinely. Prayer books were burnt and missionaries were expelled from Vietnam. The proscription was especially severe under the Tây-so'n, perhaps because the Tây-so'n were fighting against the Nguyễn in the south and suspected European missionaries of being the secret agents of their rivals.

At the end of the eighteenth century, Nguyễn Ánh by the care of Bishop of Adran asked help from France against the Tây-so'n. However, after defeating these and proclaiming himself the Emperor Gia-long, he proved to be little appreciative of French culture, since as a matter of fact, all of his political and social reforms were patterned after Chinese institutions. Moreover, his successors Minh-mạng, Thiệu-trị and Tụ'-đú'c were far less sympathetic than himself to the new trends coming from the West and labelled them "perverse to public order." Thus in the nineteenth century under the Nguyễn dynasty like previous one, if Vietnamese rulers were not reluctant to make good use of Western technology and Western abilities, they did so only to meet temporarily pressing needs, far from being conscious of Western cultural values. Such a behaviour toward the West can probably be explained by the root influence of Chinese culture and especially of Confucian teachings[41)].

The same Chinese influence accounts for ancient Vietnamese rulers' policy against the preaching of Christianity which, they were afraid, might throw disorder into Vietnamese society hitherto based on the principles of Confucian ethics. This attitude of self-esteem and narrow mindedness characterized the Nguyễn in so far as their response to Western influences is concerned and could be still found among some of the intellectuals even after France's conquest of Vietnam. It was to last on until the beginning of the twentieth century when it was strongly shaken by important events in such neighbouring countries as China and Japan. The Sino-Japanese war of 1894-95 and the defeat of the conservative China by the modernized Japan brought about the Chinese reformist movement headed by K'ang Yu-wei and Liang Ch'i-ch'ao, both of whom had sojourned in Japan. Despite failures of their movements in China, political ideology of these two Cantonese intellectuals was widespread in Vietnam and old-school scholars discovered with astonishment revolutionary trends of the West which were coming through the smuggled Chinese translations from Western writers like Montesquieu, Voltaire, Diderot, J. J. Rousseau, Thomas Huxley, Herbert Spencer, Adam Smith, and John Stuart Mill. In 1911, the revolution broke out in China under the leadership of Sun Yat-sen and from 1915 the New Thought Movement was launched, through which Western thought imbued with nationalism and humanism influenced all fields of Chinese intellectual activity. In September 1915, Hsin Ch'ing-nien (*The New Youth*), the principal journal of this movement, was published under Ch'ên Tu-hsiu. In January 1917, Ts'ai Yüan-p'ei was inaugurated as chancellor of Peking University and owing to his educational reforms based on Western ideas, the University became the cradle of the so-called Chinese Renaissance. The classical written language was attacked in favour of the spoken language. This linguistic revolution was led by Hu Shih and Ch'en. The Young China Association was reorganized in June 1918 by Li Ta-chao and others with the following stated purpose: "Our Association dedicates itself to social service under the guidance of the scientific spirit, in order to realize our ideal of creating a Young China." It began the publication of its journal Shao-nien Chung-Kuo (*Young China*). The May Fourth Movement of 1919 was primarily a student protest against the decision at Versailles concerning Shantung, but it also inaugurated an epoch in the intellectual movement. Here the ideas of new thought were closely connected with nationalism[42].

Under the influence of these various events abroad, Vietnamese patriots who, for the most part, were Confucian scholars, started changing their struggle tactics. Two main trends could be noticed among them. The one was a revolutionary movement headed by Phan Bội Châu and aimed at freeing Vietnam with Japan's assistance. The other was a reformist movement represented by Phan Châu Trinh and advocated the urging need for the country to be modernized through Western-patterned education. For that purpose, Phan Châu Trinh together with other patriots set up a school under the name of Đông-Kinh nghĩa-thục, where through the channel of Quốc-ngữ' or the romanized script, they aimed at implanting among their compatriots scientific knowledge and political concepts of the West. They also worked for the introduction of a modern way of life. Many teachers of the School were sent to the provinces where they lectured on such subjects as how to modernize the country and to save it from the foreign rule. Unfortunately, this reformist movement was not long-lived because of its meeting with rising disapproval from the French authorities. In 1908, the School was closed by a decree. Some of the staff were arrested on the charge of rebellion. Only a few succeeded in escaping to China or Japan.

In the wake of the failure of Đông-Kinh nghĩa-thục Movement which lasted only one year, other factors were to operate on the orientation of the Vietnamese toward modernization. The first one was of political inspiration. From World War I, a new policy was inaugurated in Vietnam by French Governor-General Albert Sarraut. Inclined to believe that Confucian studies were responsible for such Vietnamese uprisings as those led by Phan

Châu Trinh and Phan Bội Châu, the French authorities started reforming the civil service examinations, making Western learning rather than Confucian learning the requisite for success. At the same time, new French schools were opened such as the School of Medicine and Pharmacy, Higher School of Pedagogy, Special School of Agriculture and Sylviculture, School of Applied Sciences, School of Commerce and School of Fine Arts.

According to Prof. Vũ Quốc Thúc, up to 1956 the Western impact in the form of French colonization which ended in 1945 was rather of superficial character and narrow scope[43].

"This [Vietnam's social] structure which was built up over a period of more than ten centuries is effectively communalistic since its basis was in the village or commune. Vietnam's entire economic evolution was conditioned by the division of her population into a multitude of autonomous and insulated rural communities.

"In eighty years, the French colonial administration did not basically alter this archaic structure.... As late as 1945, rural communities still embraced more than 90 per cent of the total population of the country. This preponderance of the peasant population with its static way of life explains the existence in Vietnam of many old beliefs, traditions and superstitions and the unchanging character of the entire social organization of the country.

"The principal result of the French colonization was the expansion into new domains and the creation of a new economic system superimposed upon but not replacing the traditional structure. This new system, clearly capitalistic, was implemented by the extension and modernization of some old urban centres, the creation of new towns and the development of big agricultural and mining concessions. *But barely ten per cent of the Vietnamese population found a place in the new system and were thus directly exposed to the influence of Western civilization.*"[44)]

2. WESTERN IMPACT ON VIETNAMESE LANGUAGE AND WRITING

Western impact or more accurately the influence of the French language on the Vietnamese language dates back to as early as the beginning of the French occupation of South Vietnam. It began to operate through the first newspapers in Quốc-ngữ' like the Gia-Định Báo (1865) and the Nông-Cổ Mín-Đàm (1900). But it was after 1910 and especially after the suppression of the old triennial examination system in 1915 in North Vietnam and in 1918 in Central Vietnam that the French language gained more and more in importance. Among various contributions of the French language to the enrichment of Vietnamese language, we should lay emphasis on the French-patterned structure of some Vietnamese sentence patterns and some loanwords from French.

Before receiving influence from the French language,

the Vietnamese sentence had been modelled after the old Chinese sentence and it had been, like the latter, too much symmetrical, florid and finical. Later on, in touch with the French language through the channel of translation works, it became more simple, clear and realistic. With regard to loanwords from French, they have not been too abundant at least as far as direct borrowings are concerned. Let us mention, for instance, cuốc (course), bắc (bac), xà-lúp (chaloupe), ca-nốt (canot), ô-tô (auto) and to'-nít (tennis).

While being both discreet and relatively recent with regard to the Vietnamese language, Western impact, on the other hand, proved to be more apparent and of longer standing as far as the Quốc-ngữ' or the Vietnamese romanized script is concerned. This new Vietnamese script had been, for the first time, used by Alexandre de Rhodes in his Vietnamese-Portuguese-Latin dictionary. However, the history of its invention was not all clear. In any case, many missionaries of various nationalities might have contributed to it. Effectively, the system shows traces of the spelling habits of such languages as Portuguese, Spanish, French and Italian. Moreover, it has likely had more or less connection with the first attempts to romanize such Asian languages as Japanese and Chinese. As a matter of fact, in 1548 the *Romaji* or the romanized script of Japanese was practised for the first time by Yajiro, a Japanese missionary. Later on, in 1626, Nicholas Trigault, another famous missionary, published his lexicographical work entitled Hsi-ju êrh-mu-tzŭ, in which the Chinese language was romanized for the first time. At first, the romanized script was used only by missionaries to translate prayer books and catechisms. When they began to teach it in school after the southern part of Vietnam became the French Colony of Cochin-China in 1867, such scholars as Petrus Tru'o'ng Vĩnh Ký and Paulus Huỳnh Tịnh Của also wrote in Quốc-ngũ' to translate Chinese novels and to produce some elementary textbooks (*pl. 4*).

After the adoption of Quốc-ngũ' as the official medium of education in primary school all over Vietnam, the romanized script which gained its popularity and universality through the campaign for the diffusion of Quốc-ngũ' has acquired the full status of "national script." As a phonetic script, par excellence, the Quốc-ngũ' provides for the transcription not only of all the loanwords but all the original Vietnamese words. Through this medium, the traditional values of national literature whether they were expressed in demotic characters or written in Chinese characters could be preserved to our times. But the effective contribution of the Quốc-ngũ' is not limited exclusively to the past. It is also oriented toward the future and will certainly help to produce a literature which would be a fruitful synthesis of Eastern and Western cultures.

3. WESTERN IMPACT THROUGH THE PRESS

The press, which did not exist in Vietnam before the French occupation made its first appearance in Saigon with the Gia-Định Báo (*Gia-Dinh Newspaper*) in 1865 and in North Vietnam with the Đại-Nam Dồng-văn Nhật-báo (*Dai-Nam Daily News*). The former was published in Quốc-ngũ' and the latter in the Chinese characters. Both of them were official information papers supervised by the Protectorate Government.

Next came newspapers published by private persons, such as for South Vietnam the Nông Cổ Mín-Đàm (1900) and the Nhật Báo tỉnh (1905) and for North Vietnam the Đậi-Việt Tân-Báo (1905) which was written both in Quốc-ngũ' and in Chinese characters. In 1907, the Đại-nam Dồng-văn Nhật-báo took the supplementary name of Đăng Cổ tùng báo and included a supplement in Vietnamese. Its chief editor was Nguyễn Văn Vĩnh. All these papers aimed at publishing nothing but daily news and circular notices. From 1910 to about 1934, besides such daily newspapers as the Lục-Tỉnh Tân-văn (1910), Trung-Bắc Tân-văn (1915), Thụ'c-Nghiệp Dân-báo (1920), Trung-Lập-báo (1923), there were also literary, scientific and artistic magazines. Literary magazines like the Đông-Du'o'ng Tạp-chí (1913), the Nam-Phong Tạp-chí (1917), the Đại-Việt Tạp-chí (1918), the Hũ'u-Thanh Tạp-chí (1921), the An-nam Tạp-chí (1926) intended to popularize Eastern and Western cultural values through the channel of Quốc-ngũ'. Among the most famous scientific and artistic magazines of this period, let us mention the Học-Báo (1919), the Khoa-học Tạp-chỉ (1931), the Khoa-học phổ-thông (1934), the Bảo-an y-báo (1934), the Chó'p bóng (1932) and the Loa (1934).

Of all the above-mentioned magazines, the most prominent ones with regard to the impact of Western culture have been unquestionably the Đông Du'o'ng Tạp-chí and the Nam-Phong Tạp-chí. One of the main activities of these two magazines was to endeavour to introduce and popularize Western culture by writing many articles on them or by translating works of Western sciences and humanities into Vietnamese language.

From 1935 to 1945 the Vietnamese press was in full swing and, as one of its new characteristics, more emphasis was laid on political considerations. That is why, apart from literary magazines and information papers, many politico-cultural organs were also published, such as the Ngày Nay (*The Present Times*) in 1935, the Nam-Cu'ò'ng (*Vietnam's Strength*) in 1938, the Tin-Tú'c (*Information Magazine*) in 1938, the Cấp-Tiến (*Radical Party*) in 1938. The most influential among these has been the Ngày Nay. It was a new organ of the politico-literary group Tụ'-Lụ'c Văn-Đoàn from 1935 to 1940. It was set up as early as 1932 and headed by the writer Nhất Linh. It included as its principal members such writers as Khái Hu'ng, Thế Lũ' and Tú Mõ'. Among its achievements, as far as the Western impact is concerned, we should mention the so artistically written novels in which individual freedom was shielded from the big family's oppression; translations of famous works of French, American, British and Russian literatures into Vietnamese; Western-patterned styles of writing such as play-writing and modern poetry; and, always along the same line, the initiative of the reform of women's clothes. In a word, it had revived the thought and the modernist movement which were advocated by many intellectuals and revolutionaries since 1920. Simultaneously other literary circles and magazines contributed more or less to the spreading of Western cultural values in Vietnam. Finally, from 1945 to 1954, during the resistance against the second French occupation, there occurred a pause off in the cultural exchange between Vietnam and the West which was not to be reopened until after 1954.

4. WESTERN IMPACT ON VIETNAM THROUGH TRANSLATIONS

Next to the schools and the press, translations of Western works into Vietnamese have been perhaps the most efficient auxiliary of the Western impact on Vietnamese culture. The first Vietnamese translation of Western works dates back to the seventeenth century when Alexandre de Rhodes published his bilingual Latin-Vietnamese catechism in Rome. But it was only in the beginning of the nineteenth century that Latin-Vietnamese and French-Vietnamese translations were found published again for the most part in the form of bilingual dictionaries.

In the course of the period running from the first quarter of the nineteenth century to the beginning of the twentieth century, most of the translators were Catholic missionaries and it is obvious that their primary motive was a religious one. The earliest of their works was produced by a French missionary, Bishop of Taberd, who in 1838 was the first to give English, French and Vietnamese translations of a Latin poem about the martyrdom of Agnes (Agnetis Martyrium). Then other missionaries followed his process. Their translation programme necessarily laid emphasis on religious works like Sacred Scripture, theology, hagiography and rituals. However, translations of Latin and French textbooks also retained their attention.

During the last years of the nineteenth century and the first years of the twentieth century, translation of Western works grew more and more in importance and began to interest Vietnamese intellectuals themselves. The most active translators then were Tru'o'ng Vĩnh Ký (1837–1898) and Huỳnh Tịnh Của (1834–1907) in the south and shortly after, Nguyễn Văn Vĩnh and Phạm Quỳnh in the north. Tru'o'ng Vĩnh Ký, a polyglot scholar, was the author of numerous works covering various subjects, such as old legends, humorous tales, Vietnamese grammar, Vietnamese history and accounts of travel. However, he was most appreciated for his French-Vietnamese and Vietnamese-French dictionaries as well as for his translations from Chinese, Latin and French. Huỳnh Tịnh Của, one of his contemporary scholars, was also known especially for his Western-patterned tales and his Vietnamese dictionary entitled Đại-Nam Quấc-âm tự'-vị. The period from 1913 to 1932 was, so to speak, the golden age of the translation of Western works, and was represented by two eminent translators: Nguyễn Văn Vĩnh and Phạm Quỳnh. The former's translations covered various kinds of Western literary works with special emphasis on novels and comedies. Let us mention for instance *Les Fables* by La Fontaine, *Les Contes de la Mère l'Oye* by Perrault, *Les Vies parallèles des hommes illustres de la Grèce et de Rome* by Plutarque, *Gil Blas de Santillane* and *Turcaret* by Lesage, *Gulliver's Travels* by Jonathan Swift, *Les Aventures de Télémaque* by Fénelon, *Les Trois mousquetaires* by Alexandre Dumas, *Manon Lescaut* by Abbé Prévost, *La Peau de chagrin* by Honoré de Balzac, *Les Misérables* by Victor Hugo and *Le Malade imaginaire, Le Bourgeois gentilhomme, L'Avare, Le Tartuffe* by Molière. Most of these translations were to be reissued in the collection named Âu-Tây Tu'-tu'ở'ng (*The Western Thought*) which was initiated in 1927 by Nguyễn Văn Vĩnh and Vayrac.

Phạm Quỳnh's translations showed a clear preference for works of ethics and philosophy. Such as *Le Discours de la méthode* by Descartes, *Le Manuel* by Epictète, *La Vie sage* by Paul Carton. Nevertheless, he also translated French novels like *Le Rouge et le noir* by Stendhal, French tragedies like *Le Cid* and *Horace* by Corneille.

Moreover, he was the author of such numerous compilations on various fields of Western cultures as Văn-minh-luận (*Essay on Civilization*), Khảo về chính-trị nu'ó'c Pháp (*Studies in Political Institutions of France*), Thế-gió'i tiến-bộ sủ' (*History of the World's Progress*), Lịch-sủ' và học-thuyết của Rousseau (*Rousseau's Biography and Doctrine*), Lịch-sủ' và học-thuyết của Montesquieu (*Montesquieu's Biography and Doctrine*) and Lịch-sủ' và học-thuyết của Voltaire (*Voltaire's Biography and Doctrine*).

Apart from Nguyễn Văn Vĩnh and Pham Quỳnh, we should mention such translations of works by other writers as published in the Đông-Du'o'ng Tạp-chí Magazine, in the French supplement to Nam-Phong Tạp-chí Magazine, and in the bulletin of the Society of Mutual Education of Tonkin[45)] headed by Nguyễn Văn Tố. From 1932 to 1945. Translations from Western literature kept on being an important field of Vietnamese intellectual activity. However, some changes could be observed in their orientation. More attention was given to other Western literatures than French literature and, with regard to the latter, preference was shown for modern authors rather than for classical ones.

Under the influence of Western masterpieces translated by such writers as Tru'o'ng Vĩnh Ký and others, Vietnamese prose became richer, expressing its ideas in new ways and grew in fame with the production of various valuable works, such as novels, theatrical plays and criticism. Vietnamese poetry also kept pace with this

Western trend in Vietnamese prose and was given fresh lustre by such remarkable poets as Nguyễn Khắc Hiếu, Trần Tuấn Khải and Đông Hồ. Finally, let us point out again the role of the Vietnamese press which through their original writings and their translations of Chinese or French works greatly contributed to the growth and enrichment of the Vietnamese literature in Quốc-ngữ'[46].

5. WESTERN IMPACT ON ARCHITECTURE, PAINTING AND MUSIC

As far as Vietnamese arts are concerned, Western impact has been also very important. It has been, according to Prof. Phạm Biểu Tâm, *"on the whole quite positive"*[47] in architecture, painting and music.

Western impact on Vietnamese architecture dates back as early as to the beginning of the Nguyễn dynasty and was revealed by such structures as the Hoàng-thành (Imperial City), and fortification in Vauban's manner built with the cooperation of the French military officers who gave their assistance to Nguyễn Ánh against the Tây-so'n. But it was during and after the reign of Emperor Khải-định (1916–25) that the Western influence on Vietnamese architecture began to show the considerable increase (*pl. 1*). The influence of French architecture superseded then that of the Chinese and the neoclassical style which was all the rage in France about the beginning of the twentieth century attempted vainly to get acclimatized to Indochina as evidenced by the Imperial Villa gate in An-định. Nowadays, Western impact on Vietnamese architecture is increasing on an ever larger scale, especially in the urban centres.

French patterns started influencing Vietnamese painting from 1923 when the French School of Fine Arts was founded in Hanoi with the participation of such artists as Tardieu, a painter, Jonchère, a sculptor, and Inguimberty, an artist-decorator. The first Vietnamese artists to introduce Western fine arts, especially Western styles of paintings, into Vietnam were Lê Phổ, Mai Trung Thứ and Vũ Cao Đàm. A number of these pioneers boldly adopted Western oil painting technique while some others continued to practise the traditional technique of silk painting. Later on, from about 1944, a new creative spirit has taken shape in Vietnamese painting and gave birth to various masterpieces such as cubist paintings of Tạ Tỵ, silk prints of Tú Duyên, and silk paintings of Trần Văn Thọ. Recently, many painters, after improving their technique in Europe, have brought back with them various concepts of the Western neoplastic. At the same time, together with other artists in the country, they have been feverishly working to build up Vietnamese painting on new basis.

Western impact on Vietnamese music dates back to World War I, about the same time as the rise of Hát-cải-lương or renovated theatre in South Vietnam. After the first successful attempts by such artists as Nguyễn Văn Tề, Năm Châu, Ái Liên and Kim Thoa, the movement for music renovation gained ground more and more over the country. Enthusiasm for Western music reached its climax between 1932 and 1939. Many modern musical scores were published in the Phong-Hóa literary magazine (1932–35) by such artists as Nguyễn Văn Tuyên, Nguyễn Xuân Khoát, and Lê Thu'o'ng. In 1939, other ones were all the rage, such as Khúc-bản Ca-chiều (*Serenade*) by Văn Chang, Biệt-ly (*Farewell*) by Dzoãn Mẫn, Đôi-oanh-vàng (*The Two Orioles*) by Thẩm Oánh, Tâm-hồn anh tìm em (*My Soul Seeking You*) by Du'o'ng Thiệu Tu'ó'c and Buồn-tàn-thu (*Sadness in Late Autumn*) by Văn Cao.

From 1941 new trends could be found in many songs inspired by patriotism and heroism. A group of students at Hanoi University materialized them in their new productions the most characteristic of which were represented by Tiếng-gọi Thanh-niên (*Appeal to the Youth*), Sông Bạch-dằng (*Bach-dang River*). Finally, from 1945 to now, Vietnamese modern music has realized many other achievements some of which were also appreciated abroad. With regard to music teaching, we should mention the activities of Saigon National Conservatoire which has set itself the task of renovating Vietnamese music on the basis of a new synthesis of East and West.

6. WESTERN IMPACT ON ECONOMIC, SOCIAL AND FAMILY LIFE

Under the Western impact especially in the form of French culture which was spread by the schools, the press and the radio, the traditional social framework of Vietnam slowly crumbled in the urban areas. As early as 1920, there were evident clear tendencies toward the emancipation of the individual from the restrictions of traditional institutions. From 1920 to about 1940, the success of romanticism in Vietnamese literature seemed to symbolize an over-emphasis on individual concepts. However, a change of attitude occurred after this period. The notion of individual interests began to give way gradually during the forties in favour of the social concept which has been exploited by the communists in their rule over North Vietnam since 1954, while it has been inspiring South Vietnam in her struggle for freedom and democracy.

It is rather a minority that has been influenced by Western practices, while the rural population was kept aloof from any foreign influences. In all urban centres, housing conditions have been altered considerably and Western architecture has almost entirely replaced traditional structures. Vietnamese furniture have also been influenced greatly by Western contacts. It was either superseded by Western style pieces or was only kept for decorative purposes. Clothing has been modernized with the same facility. Most men in town have adopted Western costume. Traditional dress and trousers are rarely worn by students and schoolboys, whose uniforms generally consist of a white shirt, a pair of trousers and a pair of shoes or sandals, all being cut in Western style. Girls and women prefer having their hair cut and curled in Western fashion. With respect to means of transportation, Vietnamese have freely adopted the use of modern vehicles. Even women can be seen now driving cars and riding bicycles or motor scooters. As for recreational pursuits and the sports, the movies, tennis, football and boxing have won over Vietnamese youth.

Thus Western impact has been effective on the Vietnamese way of life especially in the urban area. Nevertheless, as rightly stated Prof. Vũ Quốc Thúc, "it would seem that Western influence has been irregular, its importance varying from one aspect to another. There has been on the part of Vietnamese city-dwellers neither a stubborn rejection nor a hasty adoption. Instead, Vietnam has taken from the West what she thought best suited to her comfort, pleasure and taste. Westernization has taken place, in other words, according to a thoroughly rational pattern."[48]

CHAPTER VI

CONCLUSION

In the preceding chapters, we have tried to trace back various contributions of Eastern and Western cultures to Vietnamese culture in the process of its formation. If we set aside such constituents as Hoabinhian and Bacsonian cultures which date back to the prehistoric era, Vietnamese culture from the Christian era up to now has been successively moulded by Austro-Asiatic culture, Indian culture, Chinese culture and Western culture.

The importance of alien constitutive elements in Vietnamese culture had led to the tempting hypothesis that the Vietnamese culture is, after all, no more than a provincial variant of Chinese culture. This hypothesis has been disapproved by A. H. Christie. He said that the culture of the Vietnamese developed in a distinctly Chinese pattern. Yet, from a careful analysis of the earliest surviving evidence and detailed comparative studies of regional cultures, it is possible to show that the naïve view which holds Vietnamese culture to be no more than provincial Chinese is over-simplified and untenable[49].

Thus, despite the overpowering impact of Chinese

culture, Vietnamese culture should not be considered only a variety of Chinese culture. Nor should it be identified with Indian culture although many elements of which can yet be traced through some present Vietnamese cultural patterns.

Apart from these two views which hold Vietnamese culture to be an impoverished version either of Chinese culture or of Indian culture, we should also mention a new hypothesis which attempted to identify Vietnamese culture with Austro-Asiatic culture. According to Dr. Condominas, "the virile originality of Vietnam emerges in all spheres. Certainly, there is no question of minimizing Chinese influence, which has been preponderant, but not so absolute, as most works intended for the general public seemed to give the impression that the cultural personality of Vietnam had been suffocated by Chinese culture, of which it was alleged to be nothing more than an integral part. It is undeniable that there was a Chinese cultural influence on Vietnam just as there was elsewhere an Indian influence. But that ancient cultural substratum which is common to the peoples of Southeast Asia, a crossroad for both Indian and Chinese cultures, has survived intact with the remote minority mountaineers. Moreover, it has also profoundly tinged the language, customs, manners, social organization, arts and beliefs of modern Vietnam. It will absorb all the opposing currents of Western world just as it gratuitously absorbed or accepted by force the multiple elements of Chinese culture and made use of them to build up its own culture and to maintain its own originality."[50]

While recognizing that the previous opinion has rightly taken into account such main constituents of Vietnamese culture as Chinese, Indian and especially Austro-Asiatic cultural patterns, we are inclined to think, however, that the originality of Vietnamese culture lies rather elsewhere than in its Austro-Asiatic substratum. It is likely to be seen in the synthesis that it has realized of native and exogenous elements. This synthesis has been materialized more or less successfully as evidenced above, in almost every sphere of Vietnamese culture.

APPENDIX

I. TAM AND BODHISATTVA

Many centuries ago there lived a happy couple, and a beautiful daughter was born to them. But as if charging a price for giving the couple such a beautiful daughter, nature took away the mother as soon as the girl was born. The girl was named Tấm by her father who was torn between grief and joy. But time passed heedlessly, and the father decided to marry again. From the second marriage another daughter was born, whom they named Cám. All the four lived together. Tấm loved her little half sister, but was hated by her stepmother. In the midst of love and hate, the two girls grew up.

One day the stepmother sent two girls to bring shrimps from a nearby pond. Tấm worked hard; Cám was too spoilt to work, and played with the flowers and butterflies. When the time came to return home, Cám seeing Tấm's full basket, felt a little apprehensive of her reception at home. But a scheme took shape in her mind, and she exclaimed to Tấm, "My goodness, just look at your hair and face! Go and wash!" Tấm put the basket down and scampered away to clean herself. When she returned, the shrimps were of course not there. Neither was Cám. Tấm sat down and began to cry.

While she was crying, someone touched her shoulder.

She did not know it, but it was a Bodhisattva. He asked in a gentle voice, "Why are you crying, my child?" Tấm told him the story, and said: "My mother will beat me to death when she finds I've brought no shrimps." Bodhisattva replied, "Child, do not cry. If you endure your suffering now, you will be happy later." Then he asked her to look into her basket, and there was a small fish in it. "Take this fish," he said, "and put it in the pond."

This Tấm did. And everyday, instead of eating all her three bowls of rice, she would keep one for the fish. She would go to the pond and call "Fish, Fish!" and the fish would come to surface and eat out of her hand. It soon became big, beautiful and playful. But how could this happiness be concealed from the curious eyes of Cám? One day, Tấm called the fish, with food on her hand, but the fish did not come up. It never came up any more.

So Tấm sat down and cried again, quietly, near the pond. And again the Bodhisattva appeared before her, and asked, "Why are you crying, child?" She sobbed out her loss. The Bodhisattva said, "The fish was caught and eaten. Its bones are in the garden. Gather them, and bury them under the four legs of your bed." Then he left. When she went to the garden, Tấm found a cock scratching the earth very hard. Sure enough, she found there the bones of the fish. She did as Bodhisattva had advised.

Some time after, there was a big festival in the vicinity which the King was going to grace with his presence. Everybody in the village was going, and there was much excitement. Tấm also was excited, and wished to go. But the stepmother, though she allowed Cám immediately, told Tấm to finish some work before going. She took two jars of black and green peas, mixed them, and put the whole lot in front of Tấm. "You can go to the festival after you have separated the black from the green peas," she said. And the family left for the festival.

Tấm sat alone, looking at the heap of peas before her. She began to separate them and tears flowed silently from her eyes as she worked. Then the Bodhisattva again appeared. "Crying again, child?" he asked. Tấm pointed at the mixed peas and said: "I can never go to the festival." The Bodhisattva consoled her, and thought for a moment. Then he looked up and thence flew down hundreds of little birds which separated the green from the black peas in a few minutes. "There!" said the Bodhisattva. "*Now* you can go." Tấm was full of joy. But she suddenly remembered that she had nothing to wear. But the Bodhisattva advised her to dig under the bed, where she had buried the fishbones. There she found beautiful garments, and she dressed to leave.

When she was on the bridge, the King arrived. The guards unceremoniously asked everybody to clear out of the way, and as she hurried to one side, she dropped one of her shoes. It lay there for some time. Then one of the guards saw it, and was attracted by a strange, undefinable quality of it, and by its beauty. It did not seem to him to have been made by a human hand —it wasn't, of course. So he took it to the captain, who conveyed it to the King. The King was also struck with wonder. He wished to know which lady's shoe it was, but no one stepped forward to tell him. Then he proclaimed that whomsoever the shoe fitted would become his queen. All the ladies tried, including Cám; when her foot was found too big for it, her mother was so enraged with envy. Ultimately, Tấm also had to try, and she of course became the queen. Her mother and her half sister would never forgive her, for they were very jealous of her.

Many years passed. One day, Tấm heard that her father was ill, and she returned home to see him. While she was there, her stepmother thought of a ruse and asked her to climb up and get some areca nut for her father. Although she was a queen—and queens *don't* normally climb trees—she went up. When she was well up, Cám and her mother, who had cut sufficiently deep into the trunk before sending Tấm up, now quickly cut the tree down. Tấm fell, and died. The Bodhisattva transformed her into a yellow bird.

In the meantime, Cám went to the palace as a substitute. One day she was drying the King's clothes, when a yellow bird came fluttering around and said, "Do not dry my husband's garments on the fence—they will tear, they will tear!" As destiny wanted, the King was standing nearby, amazed to hear this. Then he raised his hand and said, "Yellow bird, yellow bird, if you are my wife, get into the sleeve of my robe!" The yellow bird of course flew in. The King loved the bird, and made a home for it in the palace. But Cám could not stand. At the first opportunity that came, she killed the bird and threw its feathers into the garden. The wind carried the feathers away and where it deposited them there grew up a luxuriant tree with just one beautiful fruit. A beggar-woman, passing by, saw the fruit, and opening her bag, said, "Fruit, beautiful fruit, fall into my bag. I'm not going to eat you, I shall keep you in my house." Immediately the fruit fell into the bag. The beggar-woman brought it home and the house was immediately filled with fragrance. She kept it in the rice jar.

But from the day she brought the fruit, a strange thing happened. Everytime she returned from her rounds, she found the housework done, and her meal ready and served. She couldn't find out how, so she decided to investigate. One day she hid outside the house and watched. She saw emerging from the jar a beautiful lady who began to do the housekeeping. The beggar-woman rushed in and caught her by the arm. After she had learnt as much as the lady told her, the two began to live quietly together.

It chanced one day that the King came that side for hunting. Tired, he stopped at the woman's place for some betel leaves and a drink of water. When the betel leaf was brought to him, he was surprised to find that it had been made in the way that his wife used to make it for him. So he inquired from the old woman, and she told him it had been made by her daughter. The King summoned the "daughter" and when she came, he could only stare: she was the image of his wife. He asked her all about herself, and she told him the whole story. The King's joy was boundless, and she went back with him to the palace in full glory, to live happily ever after.

II. THE BUFFALO BOY

On a clear night, if you look at the moon intently, the pattern on its surface will play all kinds of tricks: sometimes its corners will round to curves, and its curves to corners; sometimes it will approximate to this known shape, sometimes to that. But if you continue to look, the movement will gradually cease, and the silhouette will emerge of a man sitting all alone at the foot of a banyan tree. The man's name is Cuội, and he went up to the moon long, long ago. But the children of Vietnam still sing of him when they see the moon and sometimes they are sure that he turns his head to look at them and smile. And they sing:

Cuội, Cuội, the dream-time boy,
Alone, alone on the Moon,
Playing with the stars in the lost twilight
Till Late has become Soon.

Cuội was a buffalo-boy who came of a very, very poor family. Because he was so poor, he worked without being paid for the richest man in his little world. He used to look after the buffalo in the fields, prepare food for the pigs, collect firewood in the forest, and cook dinner for his master. For all this, the master used to give food to eat, a cloth to cover himself with, and a box on the ear to encourage him.

One day, while gathering wood in the forest, Cuội saw a tiger-cub come frolicking up to him. He picked it up. As he did so, he heard a frightful growl somewhere close by. The mother of the cub was looking for her little one. Cuội threw the cub down and scrambled up to hide in a tree. But he had thrown down the cub with such violence that it lay unconscious. The tigress soon came crashing through the undergrowth, and growled again—this time with anger. In the tree, Cuội held his breath with difficulty. Then Cuội saw a strange thing happen. The tigress walked to a stream not far from the spot, gathered leaves from a tree which looked like a banyan, chewed them, and applied them to the cub's head. The cub almost immediately stood up and jumped about as if nothing had happened.

When the tigress and her little one had disappeared into the forest, Cuội came down and made his way to the banyan tree. He gathered a handful of leaves and took them home. On the way he saw a dog lying dead in the dust. Cuội chewed the leaves as he had seen the tigress doing, and applied them to the dog's head. After a few minutes the dog came to life again, and bounded away. Realizing that these leaves had the strange property of bringing the dead back to life, Cuội returned to the stream and brought away the whole tree complete with its roots. He replanted the tree at his house, in the middle of the yard, and warned his wife not to throw refuse and dirty water where it was planted. "Otherwise," he joked, "the tree will fly away to the sky."

But Cuội's wife was like the other village women of Asia; how could she remember where not to throw refuse and dirty water? She threw these things just where Cuội had asked her not to throw them. Slowly the tree began to pull itself out, and make towards the sky. Somehow, the joke was coming true. Cuội, returning from the fields, saw the tree floating away, to his horror. He ran after it, as if he were mad, and just caught hold of its roots. But his slight weight was not sufficient to keep the tree down, and he too was carried up. After many hours, the tree and Cuội reached a strange world, with a permanent after-storm calm. It was the Moon. Cuội planted the tree there, and sat down to wait at its foot. And there he has sat waiting, year after year, for Late to become Soon.

Excerpts from Dỗ Vạng Lý: *The Stork and the Shrimp,* (The Claw of the Golden Turtle and Other Vietnamese Tales), New Delhi, 1959.

NOTES

1. G. Coedès: *Les Peuples de la péninsule indochinoise. Histoire des Civilisations,* pp. 17-32. D.G. E. Hall: "Looking at Southeast Asian History," *Journal of Asian Studies,* XIX/3, p. 244. Nguyễn Văn Thái and Nguyễn Văn Mù'ng: *A Short History of Viêt-Nam,* pp. 3-8. Gene Gregory, Nguyễn Lâu and Phan Thị Ngọc Quó'i: *A Glimpse of Viêt-Nam,* pp. 13-23. *Republic of Vietnam; Country Study,* pp. 19-32.
2. Lin Yü-tang: *My Country and My People,* pp. 169-170.
3. Nguyễn Đăng Thục: *Democracy in Traditional Vietnamese Society,* p. 9. (Vietnam Culture Series No. 4).
4. Đại-Việt sủ'-ký ngoại-kỷ toàn-thu', k. 5, Ngô kỷ.
5. Nguyễn Văn Thái and Nguyễn Văn Mù'ng: *op. cit.,* pp. 70-170, 225-238.
6. Jean Herbert: *Introduction à l'Asie,* p. 39.
7. Khâm-định Việt-sủ' thông-giám cu'o'ng-mục, Tiền-biên, k. 2. Trần Trọng Kim: Việt-Nam sủ'-lu'ọ'c, p. 50.
8. Duke of Chou, son of King Wên, founder of the Chou dynasty. He served as regent to his nephew, King Chêng (r. 455-418 B.C.) and attained remarkable success in suppressing the large-scale rebellion. To him was attributed the foundation of the sys-

tems of inheritance, cult of ancestors, mourning ceremony as well as the Chinese feudal system. He built the state of Lu where Confucius was born. Confucius and his followers found in him an ideal personality both in moral and in practice.

9. Trần Trọng Kim: *op. cit.*, p. 435. Tru'o'ng Văn Bình: "Customs of Vietnam," *The Times of Vietnam Magazine,* III/25, p. 3.
10. Edouard Chavannes: *Mémoire sur les religieux eminents par I-tsing,* p. 8.
11. Henri Maspero: "Quelques mots annamites d'origine chinoise," BEFEO, XVI/3, pp. 35-39. "Le dialecte de Tch'ang-ngan sous les T'ang," BEFEO, XX/2, p. 21.
12. English translation by Prof. Nguyễn Đình Hòa.
13. Tru'o'ng Văn Bình: *op. cit.,* II/31, p. 16.
14. Trần Văn Khê: *La Musique vietnamienne traditionnelle,* p. 8.
15. Lê Tắc: An-Nam chí-lu'ọ'c, p. 31.
16. Đại-Việt sủ'-ký bản-kỷ toàn-thu', k. 7, Trần kỷ.
17. Trân Văn Giáp: "Le bouddhisme en Annam, des origines au XIIIe siècle," BEFEO, XXXII, p. 209.
18. Wu-Chi, k. 4. San-kuo-chi (*History of Three Kingdoms*), k. 49.
19. Sylvain Lévi: "Notes chinoises sur l'Inde. Le pays de Kharostra et l'écriture Kharostri," BEFEO, IV, p. 559. Maurice Durand: "L'introduction du bouddhisme au Viêt-Nam, Présence du bouddhisme, sous la direction de René de Berval," *France-Asie,* XVI,

p. 797.

20. Trần Văn Giáp: *op. cit.*
21. Pháp-vũ thụ'c-lục.
22. E. Souvignet: *Les Origines de la langue annamite,* pp. 190-203.
23. Louis Bezacier: *L'Art vietnamien,* pp. 181-187. A. H. Christie: "The Ancient Cultures of Indochina," *Asian Culture,* II/2, pp. 60-63.
24. Chou Hsiang-kuang: *Indo-Chinese Relations,* pp. 3-5.
25. Khâm-định Việt-sủ' thông-giám cu'o'ng-mục, Chính-biên, k. 3.
26. Ernest Kuhn: *Beiträge zur Sprachenkunde Hinter-Indiens.* K. Himly: *Über die einsilbigen Sprachen des Südöstlichen Asiens.*
27. Henri Maspero: "Etudes sur la phonétique historique de la langue annamite. Les initiales," BEFEO, XII/1, pp. 1-15.
28. E. Souvignet: *op. cit.*
29. André G. Haudricourt: "La place du Vietnamien dans les langues austro-asiatiques," *Bulletin de la Société de Linguistique de Paris,* XLIX/1, pp. 122-128.
30. Nguyễn Đình Hòa: *The Vietnamese Language,* pp. 5-7. (Vietnam Culture Series No. 2).
31. Nobuhiro Matsumoto: *Le Japonais et les langues austro-asiatiques,* pp. 35-40. Charles Kenneth Parker: *A Dictionary of Japanese Compound Verbs,* pp. xxvi-xxix.

32. Đại-Việt sử'-ký ngoại-kỷ toàn-thu', k. 1, Hồng Bàng kỷ.
33. Kao Hsiung-chêng: An-nan chih-yüan, k. 1. Pierre Huard and Maurice Durand: *La Connaissance du Viêt-Nam,* p. 177.
34. Đại-Việt sử'-ký ngoại-kỷ toàn-thu', k. 1, Hồng Bàng kỷ.
35. Lu'o'ng Đú'c Thiệp: Xã-hội Việt-Nam, II, pp. 240-243.
36. *Ibid.*, p. 360.
37. Đại-Việt sử'-ký bản-kỷ toàn-thu', k. 2, Lý kỷ.
38. Robert Lingat: *Les Régimes matrimoniaux du Sud-Est de l'Asie,* I, pp. 105-107.
39. Alexandre de Rhodes: *Relatione de felici successi della fede nel regno di tunchino*; *Catechismus pro ijs qui volunt suscipere baptismum in octo dies divisus*; and *Dictionarium Annamiticum, Lusitanum et Latinum.*
40. Compagnie de Chine pour la propagation de la foi et l'établissement du commerce.
41. Nguyễn Văn Thái and Nguyễn Văn Mù'ng: *op. cit.,* pp. 300-322.
42. See Tatsuro and Sumiko Yamamoto: "The Anti-Christian Movement in China," *The Far-Eastern Quarterly,* XII/2, pp. 136-137.
43. Vũ Quốc Thúc: *L'Economie communaliste du Viet-nam,* pp. 178-189.
44. Vũ Quốc Thúc: "The Influence of Western Civilization on Economic Behaviour of the Vietnamese,"

Asian Culture, I/2, p. 43.

45. Société d'enseignement mutuel du Tonkin.
46. For translation works and national writings, see Nguyễn Khắc Kham *et al.*: "Bibliography on the Acceptance of Western Cultures in Vietnam from the XVIth Century to the XXth Century," *East Asian Cultural Studies,* VI/1-4, pp. 228-249.
47. *The Southeast Asian Round Table,* p. 15.
48. Vũ Quốc Thúc: "The Influence...," *Asian Culture,* I/2, pp. 49-50.
49. A. H. Christie: *op. cit.,* p. 65.
50. G. Condominas: "Panorama de la culture vietnamienne," *France-Asie,* No. 123, pp. 92-93.

TABLE OF DYNASTIES AND REGIMES IN VIETNAM

207 B.C.–111 B.C.	Triệu (capital, Phiên-ngung: Canton)
111 B.C.–39 A.D.	First Chinese Domination (under Former and Later Han dynasties)
40– 43	Tru'ng Sisters' Uprising (c. Mê-linh)
43– 544	Second Chinese Domination (under Later Han and the Six dynasties)
544– 547	Vạn Xuân kingdom (c. Long-biên)
547– 603	Period of anarchy
603– 938	Third Chinese Domination (under Sui, T'ang and the Five dynasties)
939– 944	Ngô (c. Cồ-loa)
945– 967	Period of anarchy
968– 980	Đinh (c. Hoa-lu')
981–1009	Former Lê (c. Hoa-lu')
1010–1225	Lý (c. Thăng-long: Hanoi)
1225–1400	Trần (c. Thăng-long till 1396, then Tây-đô)
1400–1407	Hồ (c. Thăng-long)
1407–1413	Later Trần (c. Thăng-long)
1413–1427	Fourth Chinese Domination (under Ming dynasty)
1428–1788	Lê (c. Đông-kinh: Hanoi)
1527–1592	Mạc's Usurpation
1532–1788	Lê's Restoration
1620–1788	Northern (Trịnh) and Southern (Nguyễn) Courts under the nominal suzerainty of Lê

	(c. Trịnh at Đông-kinh; Nguyễn at Phú-xuân: Huế since 1687)
1788–1802	Tây-so'n (c. Phú-xuân)
1802–1945	Nguyễn (c. Huế)
1867	Cochin-China under French rule
1884	French protectorate over Annam and Tonkin
1887–1945	French Indochina
1945–	Democratic Republic of Vietnam (c. Hanoi)
1954–1955	State of Vietnam (c. Saigon)
1955–	Republic of Vietnam (c. Saigon)

BIBLIOGRAPHY

Aurousseau, Léonard: "La première conquête chinoise des pays annamites au IIIe siècle avant notre ère." BEFEO,* XXIII, 137–264, 1923.

Barker, Milton: "Proto-Vietnamuong Initial Labial Consonants." VHNS, XII, 491–500, 1963.

———: "Annual Bibliographies of Far Eastern Linguistics." *Asian Perspectives,* III–VI, 1959–1963.

Baruch, Jacques: *Essai sur la littérature du Vietnam.* Casteau (Belgique), 1963.

Bekker, Konrad: "Historical Patterns of Culture Contact in Southern Asia." FEQ, XI/1, 3–15, 1951.

Bernard-Maître, Henri: *Pour la compréhension de l'Indochine et de l'Occident.* Paris, 1950.

Bezacier, Louis: *L'Art vietnamien.* Paris, 1954.

Blood, David: "A Problem in Cham Sonorants." *Zeitschrift für Phonetik,* XV, 111–114, 1962.

Blood, Doris: "Women's Speech Characteristics in Cham." AC, III, 139–143, 1961.

———: "The Y Archiphoneme in Mamanwa." AL, IV/4, 29–30, 1962.

———: "Proto-Malayo-Polynesian Reflexes in Cham." AL, IV/9, 11–20, 1962.

Blood, Evangeline: "Some Fauna Terms in a Mnong RoLom Area." VHNS, XII, 311–315, 1963.

Blood, Henry: "The Vowel System of Uon Njun Mnong Rolom." VHNS, XII, 951–965, 1963.

Boudet, Paul: *Un Voyageur philosophe Pierre Poivre*

* Key to abbreviations at the end of the *Bibliography.*

en Annam (1749–1750). Cahier de la Société de Géographie de Hanoi No. 36, 1941.

Bouteille, Michel: *Les Rapports entre la France et le Vietnam*. Paris, 1948.

Buch, W. J. M.: "La Compagnie des Indes Néerlandaises et l'Indochine." BEFEO, XXXVI, 97–196; XXXVII, 121–237, 1936–1937.

Cadière, Léopold: *Croyances et pratiques religieuses des Vietnamiens*. Paris, 1953–1957, 3 vols.

Chapman: "Narrative of a Voyage to Cochinchina in 1778." Tr. by H. Berland, BSEI, n.s., XXIII/2, 15–75, 1948.

Chapouillé, H.: *Rome et les missions d'Indochine au XVIIe siècle*. Paris, 1943–1947, 2 vols.

Chavannes, Edouard: *Voyages des pélerins bouddhistes — Les religieux éminents qui allèrent chercher la loi dans les pays d'Occident, mémoire composé à l'époque de la grande dynastie T'ang par I-tsing*. Paris, 1894.

Chou Hsiang-kuang: *Indo-Chinese Relations. A History of Chinese Buddhism*. Allahabad, U. P., India, 1955.

Christie, A. H.: "The Ancient Cultures of Indochina." AC, II/2, 51–69, 1960.

Claeys, Jean Yves: "Le Champa — L'histoire, les monuments." *Extrême-Asie,* 64, 523–534, (mai 1932).

———: "Les récentes fouilles de Tháp Mâm (Bình-Định) près de la Seconde Grande Capitale de Champa." *Extrême-Asie,* 89, 849–860, (août/sept. 1934).

Cô Chính Linh: Triết-học-khoa. Phép mộ sự' khôn ngoan (*Philosophie*). Hong Kong, 1917, 2 vols.

Coedès, G.: *Les Etats hindouisés d'Indochine et d'Indonésie*. Paris, 1948. Revised edition, 1964.

———: *Les Peuples de la péninsule indochinoise. Histoire des civilisations.* Paris, 1962.

Colani, Madeleine: *L'Âge de la pierre dans la province de Hòa-Bình (Tonkin). Mémoires du Service Géologique de l'Indochine,* XIV/1, Hanoi, 1927.

———: "La civilisation hoabinhienne extrême-orientale." *Bulletin de la Société Préhistorique Française,* XXXVI, 170–174, 1939.

———: "Fouilles à Sa-huynh et Tân-long." BEFEO, XXXIV, 755, 1934.

———: "Recherches sur le préhistorique Indochinois." BEFEO, XXX, 299–422, 1930.

Condominas, G.: "Panorama de la culture vietnamienne." FA, 123, 75–94, (août 1956).

Cordier, Georges: "Essai sur la littérature annamite." *Revue Indochinoise,* (janv. 1914), 1–36; (fév. 1914), 144–174; (mars 1914), 273–297.

———: *Etude sur la littérature annamite.* Saigon and Hanoi, 1933–1940, 3 vols.

Cordier, H.: "L'arrivée des Portuguais en Chine." *T'oung Pao,* XII, 483–543, 1911.

———: "Le journal de Pierre Poivre." *Revue d'Extrême-Orient,* 1883.

———: "Voyage de Pierre Poivre en Cochinchine." *Revue d'Extrême-Orient,* 1884.

Cuisinier, Jeanne: *La danse sacrée en Indochine et en Indonésie.* Paris, 1951.

Cultru: "Conférence sur l'occupation de la Cochinchine." BSEI, LVI, 45–61, 1909.

Cung Giũ Nguyễn: "Aperçu sur la littérature vietnamienne." Symposium in Syracuse, no. 2, 1952.

Cunningham, Alfred: "The French in Tonkin and South China." *Hong Kong Daily Press* (1902).

Dam Bo: "Les populations montagnardes du Sud Indochinois." FA, 49–50, 931–1208, 1950.

Day, Colin: "Final Consonants in Northern Vietnamese." Việt-Nam Khảo-Cổ Tập-San, III, 29–30, 1962.

Day, Colin and Hoang Van Chai: "Luc Slao-Slua" (Three Thô Legends). Saigon, 1963. (mimeo.)

D'Azy, Benoist: "L'expédition française en Cochinchine." BSEI, n.s., III/1, 25–48, 1928.

Deloustal, Raymond: "La justice dans l'ancien Annam; traduction et commentaire du Code des Lê." BEFEO, VIII, 177–220, 1908; IX, 92–122, 471–491, 765–796, 1909; X, 1–60, 349–392, 461–505, 1910; XI, 25–66, 313–337, 1911; XII/6, 1–33, 1912; XIII/5, 1–59, 1913; XIX/4, 1–88, 1919; XXII, 1–40, 1922.

Demiéville, Paul: *Le Concile de Lhasa. Une controverse sur le quiétisme entre bouddhistes de l'Inde et de la Chine au VIIIe siècle de l'ère chrétienne*. vol. I, 1952.

De Rhodes, Alexandre: *Divers voyages et missions*. Paris, 1653.

———: *Cathechismus pro ijs, qui volunt suscipere baptismum in octo dies divisus*. Phép giảng tám ngày cho kẻ muấn chịu phép rú'a tội, mà bĕào đạo thánh đú'c Chúa blò'i. Ope Sacrae Congregationis de Propaganda Fide in Lucem editus ab Alexandro de Rhodes è Sociétate IESV, eiusdemque Sacrae Congregationis Missionario Apostolico, Romae. Typis Sacrae Congregationis de Propaganda Fide Superium permissu, s.d.

Donaldson, Jean: *White Tai Phonology*. Hartford, Conn., 1963.

Dubois, Abbé J. A.: *Hindu Manners, Customs and Ceremonies*. Tr. from the author's later French M.S. and ed. with notes, corrections and bibliography by Henri K. Beauchamp. 3rd ed., Oxford, 1959.

Du'o'ng Quảng Hàm: "Le Chũ'-nôm ou écriture démotique, son importance dans l'étude de l'ancienne littérature annamite." BGIP, 7, 277–286, (mars 1942).

———: Việt-Nam Văn-Học Sử'-Yều (*Brief History of Vietnamese Literature*). Bộ Quốc-Gia Giáo-Dục. éd. de 1956.

Durand, Maurice: *Imagerie populaire vietnamienne*. Paris, 1960.

———: "Littérature vietnamienne." *Histoire des littératures*. Ed. Raymond Queneau, vol. I, 1318–1342, 1955.

———: "Alexandre de Rhodes." BSEI, n.s., XXXII, 5–30, 1957.

———: "L'introduction du bouddhisme au Viêt-Nam, Présence du bouddhism, sous la direction de René de Berval." FA, XVI/153–157, 797–800, 1959.

Đoàn Quan Tần: "L'évolution de la civilisation vietnamienne et le problème franco-vietnamien." FA, 39, 1039–1053, (juin 1949).

Đỗ Văn Minh: *Viêt-Nam Where East and West Meet*. Rome, n.d.

Đỗ Vạng Lý: *The Stork and the Shrimp*. (The Claw of the Golden Turtle and Other Vietnamese Tales). New-Delhi, 1959.

Emeneau, M.: *Studies in Vietnamese (Annamese) Gram-*

mar. Berkeley and Los Angeles, 1951.

Forrest, R. A. D.: *The Chinese Language.* London, 1948.

Gard, Richard A.: "Asian-Western Cultural Relations: Some Basic Factors." AC, I/3, 19–26, 1959.

Gaspardonne, Emile: "Matériaux pour servir à l'histoire d'Annam. I. La géographie de Li Wen-fong." BEFEO, XXIX, 63–106, 1929.

Gaudart, M.: "Les Archives de Pondichéry et les entreprises de la Compagnie française des Indes en Indochine au XVIIe siècle." *Bulletin des Amis du Vieux Hué,* 24e année/4, 353–380, 1937.

Goloubew, Victor: "L'âge du bronze au Tonkin et dans le Nord-Annam." BEFEO, XXIX, 1–46, 1929.

———: *L'Archéologie du Tonkin et les fouilles de Dông-So'n.* Hanoi, 1937.

———: "La Chine antique et l'archéologie du Tonkin; La vase Curtis au Musée du Louvre." CEFEO, 30, 23–29, 1942.

———: "Civilisation de Dong-Son dans ses relations avec l'Océanie. Le lampadaire de Lach-Tru'ò'ng." CEFEO, 25, 33–34, 1940.

———: "Report on the Making and Diffusion of Metallic Drums through Tonking and Northern-Annam." *Proceedings of IVth Pacific Science Congress, 1930,* vol. 3, 449–451.

———: "Roches gravées dans la région de Chapa (Tonkin)." BEFEO, XXV, 423–433, 1925.

———: "Sur l'origine et la diffusion des tambours métalliques." *Praehistorica Asiae Orientalis,* I, 137–150, 1932.

———: "Le tambour-génie de Đan-nê." BEFEO, XXXIII, 345–349, 1933.

———: "Le tambour métallique de Hoang-ha." BEFEO, XL, 383–409, 1940.

Gourdon, H.: *L'Art de l'Annam*. Toulouse, 1932.

Granet, Marcel: *Fêtes et chansons anciennes de la Chine*. Paris, 1929.

Gregory, Gene, Nguyễn Lâu, and Phan Thị Ngọc Quớ'i: *A Glimpse of Viêt-Nam*. Saigon, 1957.

Grousset, René: *Les Civilisations de l'Orient*. Tome II: L'Inde. Paris, 1930.

Hall, D. G. E.: "Looking at Southeast Asian History." JAS, XIX/3, 243–253, 1960.

Haudricourt, André G.: "Comment reconstruire le Chinois archaïque." *Linguistics Today,* II, 231–244, 1954.

———: "La place du Vietnamien dans les langues austro-asiatiques." *Bulletin de la Société de Linguistique de Paris,* XLIX/1, 122–128, 1953.

———: "De l'origine des tons en Vietnamien." JA, CCXLII, 69–82, 1954.

Haupers, Ralph: "Word-Final Syllabics in Stieng." VHNS, XI, 846–848, 1962.

Heine Geldern, Robert: "Prehistoric Research in Indonesia." *Annual Bibliography of Indian Archaeology,* IX, 26–38, 1934.

Herbert, Jean: *Introduction à l'Asie*. Paris, 1960.

Himly, K.: *Über die einsilbigen Sprachen des südöstlichen Asiens*. Leipzig, 1884.

Huard, Pierre: "Le noircissement des dents en Asie orientale et en Indochine." FA, 28, 804–813, (juillet

1948); 29, 906–912, (août 1948).

———: "Les Portuguais et l'Indochine." *Bulletin de l'Institut Indochinois pour l'Etude de l'Homme,* III, 47–65, 1940.

———: "Culture vietnamienne et culture occidentale." FA, 141–142, 6–21 (fév./mars 1958).

Huard, P. and Durand, Maurice: *La Connaissance du Viêt-Nam.* Hanoi, 1954.

Janse, Olov: *Archaeological Research in Indochina.* Cambridge, Mass., 1947, 1951.

———: "Viêt-Nam. Carrefour de peuples et de civilisations." FA, 165, 1645–1670, (janv./fév. 1961).

Kaeppelin, P.: *La Compagnie des Indes Orientales et François Martin.* Paris, 1908.

Karlgren, Bernhard: *The Chinese Language, an Essay on its Nature and History.* New York, 1949.

———: *Philology and Ancient China.* Oslo, 1926.

———: *Etudes sur la phonologie chinoise.* Stockholm, 1915, 4 vols.

———: "The Date of the Early Dongson Culture." *Bulletin of the Museum of Far Eastern Antiquities,* XIV, 1–28, 1942.

Kuhn, Ernest: *Beiträge zur Sprachenkunde Hinter-Indiens.* München, 1889.

Landes, A.: *Contes et légendes annamites.* Saigon, 1886.

———: *Contes Tjames.* Saigon, 1887.

Launay, A.: *Histoire générale de la Société des Missions Etrangères depuis sa fondation jusqu'à nos jours.* Paris, 1894, 3 vols.

Lavallée, A.: "Notes ethnographiques sur diverses tribus de Sud-Est de l'Indochine." BEFEO, I, 291–311,

1901.

Leclere, Jean: "De l'évolution et du développement des institutions annamites et cambodgiennes sous l'influence française." Thèse. Rennes, 1923.

Lê Tắc: An-nam chí-lược. (*Brief Description of Annam*). Ủy-ban Phiên-dịch Sử-liệu Việt-Nam. Viện Đại-Học Huế, 1961.

Lê Thành Khôi: *Le Viêt-Nam. Histoire et civilisation.* Paris, 1955.

Lê Thành Ý: "Une grande expérience intellectuelle: La culture franco-annamite." Conférence donnée à l'Université d'Hanoi le 30 avril 1942, BGIP.

Lê Văn Đàm: "Division de la littérature annamite." FA, 10, 680–681, (janv. 1947).

———: "Histoire de la littérature annamite." FA, 12, 148–150, (mars 1947); 13, 292–296, (avril 1947).

Lê Văn Hảo: "Introduction à l'ethnologie du Dình." *Revue du Sud-Est Asiatique,* 2, 173–176, 1962.

———: "Les fêtes saisonnières au Viêt-Nam." *Revue du Sud-Est Asiatique,* 4, 265–315, 1962.

Lévi, Sylvain: "Notes chinoises sur l'Inde. Le pays de Kharostra et l'écriture Kharostri." BEFEO, IV, 543–579, 1904.

Lin Yü-tang: *My Country and My People.* London, 1951.

Lingat, Robert: *Les Régimes matrimoniaux du Sud-Est de l'Asie. Essai de droit comparé indochinois.* Hanoi, Saigon, 1952, 1955, 2 vols.

Lo Ch'ang-p'ei (羅常培): "Yeh su hui shih tsai yin yün hsúeh shang ti kung hsien" (耶蘇會士在音韻學上的貢獻 (Jesuit Contribution to Chinese Phonology). *Bul-*

letin of the Institute of History and Philology, Academia Sinica, I, 267–338, 1930.

Louvet, E.: *La Cochinchine religieuse.* Paris, 1885.

Lu'o'ng Đú'c Thiệp: Xã-hôi Việt-Nam. (*Vietnamese Society*). Saigon, 1950, 2 vols.

Madrolle: *Indochina.* Paris, 1939.

Malleret, Louis: "L'art et la métallurgie de l'étain dans la culture d'Oc-Eo." *Artibus Asiae,* XIV/4, 274–284, 1948.

———: "La trace de Rome en Indochine." XXIIe Congrès International des Orientalistes, Istamboul, 1951.

———: "Les fouilles d'Oc-Eo. (1944)." BEFEO, XLV, 75–88, 1951.

———: "Aperçu de la glyptique d'Oc-Eo." BEFEO, XLIV/1, 189–199, 1944.

Marchal, Henri: *L'Architecture comparée dans l'Inde et l'Extrême-Orient.* Paris, 1944.

Maspero, Henri: *Mélanges posthumes sur les religions et l'histoire de la Chine.* Paris, 1950, 3 vols.

———: "La frontière de l'Annam et du Cambodge du VIIIe au XIVe siècle." BEFEO, XVIII/3, 29–36, 1918.

———: "Le dialecte de Tch'ang-ngan sous les T'ang." BEFEO, XX/2, 1–124, 1920.

———: "Le protectorat général d'Annam sous les T'ang. Essai de géographie historique I." BEFEO, X, 539–584, 1910.

———: "Le Royaume de Văn-lang." BEFEO, XVIII/3, 1–10, 1918.

———: "La géographie politique de l'Empire d'Annam sous les Lí, les Trần et les Hồ (IXe–XVe siècle)." BEFEO, XVI/1, 27–48, 1916.

———: "L'expédition de Ma-yuan." BEFEO, XVIII/3, 11–28, 1918.

———: "La dynastie de Lí antérieurs." BEFEO, XVI/1, 1–26, 1916.

———: "Etudes sur la phonétique historique de la langue annamite. Les initiales." BEFEO, XII/1, 1–127, 1912.

———: "Quelques mots annamites d'origine chinoise." BEFEO, XVI/3, 35–39, 1916.

Matsumoto, Nobuhiro: *Le Japonais et les langues austro-asiatiques*. Paris, 1928.

Maybon, Charles B.: *Histoire moderne du pays d'Annam (1592–1820)*. Paris, 1920.

Miller, John: "Word Tone Recognition in Vietnamese Whispered Speech." *Word,* XVII, 58–60, 1961.

Mineya, Toru: *Annango* (*Vietnamese Language*). Tokyo, 1955.

Ngan-nan tche yuan.

Nghiêm Thẩm: "La persistance culturelle du substrat indonésien chez les Vietnamiens actuels." University of Hong Kong, 1961 Golden Jubilee Congress, Symposium on Historical, Archaeological and Linguistic Studies on Southern China, Southeast Asia and the Hong Kong Region held in Hong Kong on September 11–16, 1961.

Ngô Sĩ Liên: Đại-Việt sử'-ký toàn-thu'. Vietnamese translation by Mắc Bao Thần. Hanoi, 1945.

Nguyễn Đăng Thục: "De la démocratie primaire dans la société vietnamienne." *Civilisations,* III/4, 1953.

———: *Democracy in Traditional Vietnamese Society.* English translation of the above work by Mrs.

Nguyễn Thi Hông. Saigon, 1962. (Vietnam Culture Series No. 4).
Nguyễn Đình Hòa: "Vietnamese Literature and Language." *The Times of Vietnam Magazine,* II/49, 11, 16–18, 22, 1960.
———: *The Vietnamese Language.* Saigon, 1961. (Vietnam Culture Series No. 2).
———: "Chũ'-nôm, the Demotic System of Writing in Vietnam." Reprinted from *Journal of the American Oriental Society,* LXXIX/4, 270–274, 1959.
Nguyễn Dồng Chi: Việt-Nam Cồ văn học sủ'. Hanoi, 1942.
Nguyễn Khắc Kham: Tiếng Hán Việt (*The Classical Sino-Vietnamese*).
———: "Tiếng Việt Nôm xu'a" (The Vulgar Sino-Vietnamese). Lectures at the Faculty of Letters, University of Saigon, Saigon, 1963–1964.
———: *La Littérature vietnamienne.* Saigon, 1964.
———: *Introduction to Vietnamese Culture.* Saigon, 1964. (Vietnam Culture Series No. 1).
———: "Contribution of Indian Civilization to Vietnamese Culture." *Indian Literature,* III/1, 23–27, 1959–1960.
———: *A Bibliography of Vietnamese Buddhism.* Saigon, 1963.
———: "Lu'ọ'c-sủ' công trình biên-soạn Tụ'-điền Việt-ngũ' tù' thế-kỷ thú' XVII" (Historical Survey of Lexicographical Works in Vietnam from the XVIIth Century). Lûan-Đàm Magazine, I/12, 144–148; II/1, 61–66; II/2, 222–226, 1961–1962.
———: "Vietnamese Studies and their Relationships to

Asian Studies." Paper sent to the XXVIth International Congress of Orientalists held at New-Delhi on January 4–10, 1964.
———: *Activités de la Commission Nationale Vietnamienne pour l'UNESCO*. Saigon, 1958.
———: *La République du Vietnam et la Projet Majeur Orient-Occident*. Saigon, 1959.
———: "The Acceptance of Western Cultures in Vietnam from the XVIth Century to the XXth Century." *East Asian Cultural Studies,* XI/1–4, 201–227, 1967.
Nguyễn Khac Khẩm *et al.*: "Bibliography on the Acceptance of Western Cultures in Vietnam from the XVIth to the XXth Century." *East Asian Cultural Studies,* VI/1–4, 228–249, 1967.
Nguyễn Mạnh Tu'ò'ng: "L'Annam dans la littérature française. Jules Boissière (1863–1897)." Thèse. Montpellier, 1932.
Nguyễn Phút Tân: *A Modern History of Viêt-Nam (1802–1954).* Saigon, 1964.
Nguyễn Thiệu Lâu: "Le port et la ville de Faifo au XVIIe siècle." CEFEO, 30, 11, 1942.
Nguyễn Trần Huân: *Vaste recueil de légendes merveilleuses.* Tr. from Nguyễn-Dũ"s Truyền-Kỳ Mạn-Lục. Paris, 1962.
Nguyễn Văn Huyên: *La Civilisation annamite – Connaissance de l'Indochine.* Hanoi, 1944.
———: "Introduction à l'étude de l'habitation sur pilotis dans l'Asie du Sud-Est." *Austro-Asiatica,* IV, 1934.
Nguyễn Văn Khoan: "Essai sur le Dình et le culte du génie tutélaire des villages au Tonkin." BEFEO,

XXX, 107–139, 1930.

Nguyễn Văn Liễn: "La langue annamite dans ses tendances actuelles." BSEI, n.s., IX/3, 63–73, 1934.

Nguyễn Văn Ngọc: Truyện cổ nu'ó'c Nam (*Old Stories and Legends of Vietnam*). Saigon, 1962.

Nguyễn Văn Phu'o'ng: Nghệ-thuật Việt-Nam hiện-đại (*Vietnamese Contemporary Arts*). Saigon, 1962.

Nguyễn Văn Thái and Nguyễn Văn Mù'ng: *A Short History of Viêt-Nam*. Saigon, 1958.

Oiwa, Makoto: Nhũ'ng giây liên-lạc lịch-sủ' giũ'a Nhụ't và Đông-Pháp (*Historical Relations between Japan and French Indochina*). Japan and Saigon, 1942.

Palmer-Briggs, Lawrence: "The Hinduized States of Southeast Asia." A review, FEQ, VII/4, 376–393, 1948.

Paris, Pierre: *Esquisse d'une ethnographie navale des peuples annamites*. 2e éd. Rotterdam, 1955.

Parker, Charles Kenneth: *A Dictionary of Japanese Compound Verbs*. Tokyo, 1939.

Parmentier, Henri: "Anciens tombeaux au Tonkin." BEFEO, XVII, 1–32, 1917.

Pelliot, Paul: "Deux itinéraires de Chine en Inde à la fin du VIIIe siècle." BEFEO, IV, 131–413, 1904.

Peri, N.: "Essai sur les relations du Japon et de l'Indochine aux XVIe et XVIIe siècles." BEFEO, XXIII, 1–136, 1923.

Phạm Duy Khiêm: *Légendes des terres sereines*. Paris, 1951.

Phạm Văn So'n: Việt-Nam tranh-đấu sủ'. Hanoi, 1950.

———: Việt-sử' toàn-thư' (Từ' thư'ợ'ng-cồ đến hiện tại). Saigon, 1960.

Phan Khoang: Việt-Nam Pháp-thuộc-sử' (1884–1945). Nhà sách Khai-Tri, 1961.

Phan Phát Huồn: Việt-Nam giáo-sử'. 2 parts. Saigon, 1958, 1960.

Phan Xuân Hòa: Lịch-sử' Việt-Nam (Thư'ợ'ng-cồ-Hiện-đại). Thụy-Đình, 1958.

Pittman, Richard: "Jarai as a Member of the Malayo-Polynesian Family of Languages." AC, I/4, 59–67, 1959.

———: "Southeast Asia from a Linguistic Point of View." Đại-Học Văn-Khoa, 1960.

———: "On Defining Morphology and Syntax." *International Journal of American Linguistics,* XXV, 199–201, 1959.

Republic of Vietnam: Country Study. Washington, D.C., 1959.

Reynaud: "Etude des phonèmes vietnamiens par confrontation entre le Vietnamien et quelques dialectes des Hauts-Plateaux du Sud Viet-Nam." BSEI, n.s., XXXVII/2, 117–253, 1962.

Sansom, G. B.: *Japan: A Short Cultural History.* London, 1952.

———: *Japan and the Western World.* London, 1950.

Sharp, Laurison: "Cultural Continuities and Discontinuities in Southeast-Asia." JAS, XXII/1, 3–11, 1962.

Souvignet, E.: *Les Origines de la langue annamite.* Hanoi, 1924.

Stern, Philippe: *L'Art du Champa (ancien Annam) et son évolution.* Toulouse, 1942.

Taberd, Bishop: "The Martyrdom of Agnes. Le martyre d'Agnes. Agnetis Martyrium, Inê Tử' đạo." *Dictionarium Latino-Annamiticum,* Appendix. 1838.

Taylor, Harvey: "A Phonetic Description of the Tones of the Huế Dialect of Vietnamese." VHNS, XI, 519–523, 1962.

Tchou Iun Ing (朱雲影): "中國政治制度對於日韓越的影響" *The Continent Magazine* (大陸雜誌), XXVI/1, 8–12; XXVI/2, 21–62, 1963.

Thái Văn Kiểm: "Panorama de la musique classique vietnamienne des origines à nos jours." BSEI, n.s., XXXIX/1, 53–102, 1964.

———: *Viêt-Nam Past and Present.* Saigon, 1957.

———: "Influences du Champa sur la culture vietnamienne." AC, I/1, 25–49, 1958.

The Southeast Asian Round Table. A Symposium on Traditional Cultures and Technological Progress in Southeast Asia held at Sala Santitham, Bangkok, Thailand on January 27–February 2, 1958, under the sponsorship of the Southeast Asia Treaty Organization, Bangkok.

Thịnh, Fr. Chaize (Cố): Địa-cầu vạn-vật-luận (*Histoire naturelle*). Hong Kong, 1921, 4 vols.

Thomas, David: "Các Ngữ'-tộc trong tỉnh Kontum." Văn-Hóa Á-Châu, III/1, 58–60, 1960.

———: "Basic Vocabulary in Some Mon-Khmer Languages." AL, II/3, 7–10, 1960.

———: "On Defining the 'Word' in Vietnamese." VHNS, XI, 773–777, 1962.

———: "Remarques sur la phonologie du Chrau." *Bulletin de la Société de Linguistique de Paris,* LVII/1,

175–191, 1962.

———: "Mon-Khmer Subgroupings in Vietnam" and "A Note on Proto-Viet-Mnong Tones." *Studies in Comparative Austro-Asiatic Linguistics.* Ed. N. Zide.

Thomas, Dorothy: "Proto-Malayo-Polynesian Reflexes in Rade, Jarai and Chru." *Studies in Linguistics,* XVII, 59–75, 1963.

Thompson, Laurence C.: *A Vietnamese Grammar.* Seattle, 1965.

Trần Trọng Kim: Việt-Nam sử'-lu'ọ'c (*Brief History of Vietnam*). 4th ed. Saigon, 1951.

———: Phật-giáo thu'ở' xu'a và Phật-giáo ngày nay (*Buddhism in the Past and Buddhism in the Present*). Saigon, 1953.

Trần Văn Giáp: "Le bouddhisme en Annam, des origines au XIIIe siècle." BEFEO, XXXII, 191–268, 1932.

———: "Les deux sources du bouddhisme annamite: ses rapports avec l'Inde et la Chine." CEFEO, 33, 17–20, 1942.

Trần Văn Khê: *La Musique vietnamienne traditionnelle.* Paris, 1962.

———: "Le théâtre vietnamien." *Les théâtres d'Asie.* Conférences du théâtre des Nations (1958–1959). Journées d'Etudes de Royaumont (28 mai–1 juin, 1959) réunies et présentées par Jean Jacquot. Paris, 1961.

Trivière, Léon: "Dictionnaires vietnamiens." *Bulletin de la Société des Missions Etrangères de Paris,* 2e série, XCIX, 127–140, (fév. 1957).

Tru'o'ng Bủ'u Lâm: "Introduction historique et culturelle au Viêtnam." Allocution prononcée au Palais Diên-Hông, Saigon, le 29/8/1960 à l'occasion de l'Exposition Vietnamienne.

———: "The Water Theme in Vietnamese Legends." *Proceedings of the Ninth Pacific Science Congress, 1957,* vol. 3, 114–115, 1963.

Tru'o'ng Văn Bính: "Customs of Viêtnam." *The Times of Vietnam Magazine,* II/1, 9; II/2, 13; II/3, 11–12; II/5, 7, 14; II/6, 5, 15; II/31, 16; III/6, 13; III/25, 3, 1960–1961.

Van Stein Callenfelds: "The Age of Bronze Kettledrums." *Bulletin of the Raffles Museum,* Series B, I/3.

Villars, P.: "Les Anglais au Tonkin (1672–1697)." *Revue de Paris,* 10e année/VI, 262–268, (nov. et déc. 1903).

Vũ Huy Chân: "The Popular Theatre." *The Times of Vietnam Magazine,* II/2, 10–11, 17; II/3, 9–10, 15–17; II/4, 12, 1960.

Vũ Quốc Thúc: *L'Economie communaliste du Viêt-Nam.* Hanoi, 1951.

———: "The Influence of Western Civilization on Economic Behaviour of the Vietnamese." AC, I/2, 42–53, 1958.

Yamamoto, Tatsuro and Sumiko: "Religion and Modernization in the Far East: A Symposium. II. The Anti-Christian Movement in China, 1922–1927." FEQ, XII/2, 133–147, 1953.

ABBREVIATIONS

AC: *Asian Culture*
AL: *Anthropological Linguistics*
BEFEO: *Bulletin de l'Ecole Française d'Extrême-Orient*
BGIP: *Bulletin Général de l'Instruction Publique de l'Indochine*
BSEI: *Bulletin de la Société des Etudes Indochinoises*
CEFEO: *Cahiers de l'Ecole Française d'Extrême-Orient*
FA: *France-Asie*
FEQ: *The Far Eastern Quarterly*
JA: *Journal Asiatique*
JAS: *The Journal of Asian Studies*
VHNS: Văn hóa nguyệt san

INDEX

PLATES

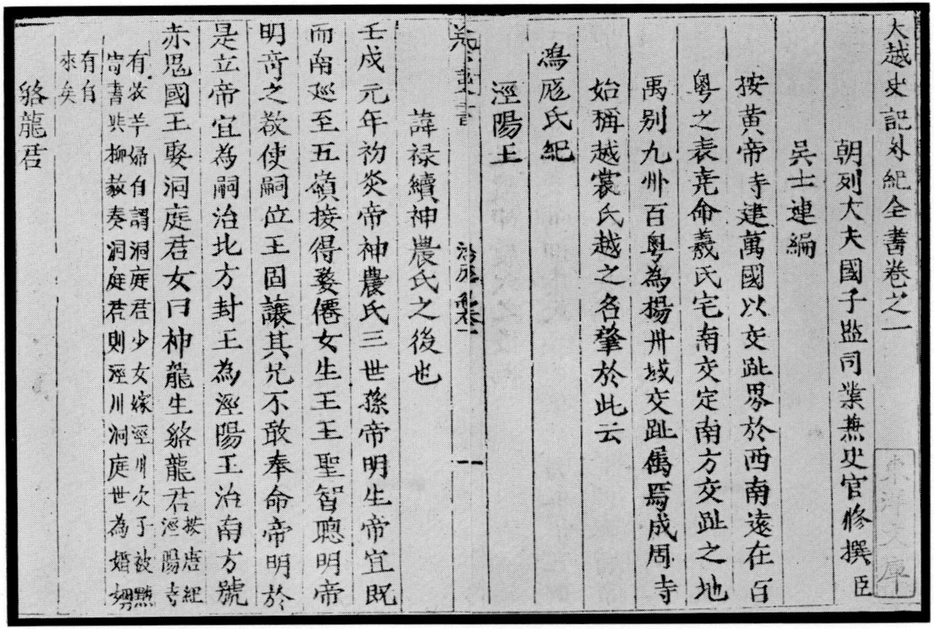

大越史記外紀全書卷之一

朝列大夫國子監司業兼史官修撰臣

吳士連編

按黃帝寺建萬國以交趾界於西南遠在百粵之表堯命羲氏宅南交定南方交趾之地禹別九州百粵為楊州域交趾屬焉成周寺始稱越裳氏越之名肇於此云

鴻厖氏紀

涇陽王

諱祿續神農氏之後也

壬戌元年初炎帝神農氏三世孫帝明生帝宜既而南巡至五嶺接得婺僊女生王王聖智聰明帝明奇之欲使嗣位王固讓其兄不敢奉命帝明於是立帝宜為嗣治北方封王為涇陽王治南方號赤鬼國王娶洞庭君女曰神龍生貉龍君按唐紀涇陽寺有牧羊婦自謂洞庭君少女嫁涇川次子被黜寄書與柳毅奏洞庭君則涇川洞庭世為婚姻有自來矣

貉龍君

1. Đại-Việt sử'-ký ngoại-kỷ toàn-thu', in literary Chinese or Chũ'-nho.

天地風塵、紅顏
多屯、悠又彼蒼
兮誰造因、
鼓鼙声動長城
月、烽火影照甘
泉雲、九重按劍
起當席、半夜飛
檄傳將軍、清平
三百年天下、從
此戎衣屬武臣、
使星天門催曉
發、行人重法輕
離別、弓箭兮在
腰妻孥兮別袂、
獨又旌旗出塞
愁、喧又簫鼓辭

2. Chinh-phụ-ngâm, both in literary Chinese (above) and in Chũ'-nôm (below).

DICTIONARIVM
ANNNAMITICVM
LVSITANVM; ET LATINVM OPE

S A C R Æ

CONGREGATIONIS
D E

PROPAGANDA FIDE
IN LVCEM EDITVM AB

ALEXANDRO DE RHODES

E Societate IESV, eiusdemque Sacræ Congregationis Missionario Apostolico.

ROMÆ, Typis, & sumptibus eiusdem Sacr. Congreg. 1651.

SVPERIORVM PERMISSV.

DICTIONARIVM
ANNAMITICVM
Seu Tunkinense cum Lusitana, & Latina declaratione.

A

á, chị á: *Irmãa primogenita*: Soror primogenita.

ác, dữ : *mao*: malus,a,um. ác nghiep: *fazer mal*: malum agere. ác tâm, lão dữ: *maos boses*: nequam. đại ác, dữ làm: *cruel*: crudelis, le. ác, chơi ác: *brincar, folgar*: ludo, is. hay ác, ác nghiep: *brincador, brincão*. lusor, oris.

ác quạ, cái ác. *coruo*: coruus, i. ác mổ, dai ác: *os coruos te comão*: corui te rodant, maledictum.

ác, thâm: *preto*: niger, a, um. gà ác *galinha preta*: gallina nigra. mèo ác: *gato preto*: fellis niger.

ác mỏ: *papagaio*: psittacus, i. ác, mỏ ác: *boca do estamago*: os ventriculi.

ách, nan: *desastre*: infortunium, ii. ngày ách: *dia*

A

aziago ou azinhago: dies ater. tóũ ách, đưa nạn: *desuiar, ò desastre*: declinare infortunium; hoc apud Ethnicos fit conuiuium faciendo diabolo &c.

ách: *iugo*: iugum, i. ách tlâu: *iugo da busara*: iugum bubali.

ai: *quem*: quis. ai đấy: *quẽ està aby*: quis est ibi. ai đi: *quem vai*: quis it. si addatur vox, có, tunc, ai, significat aliquis, vt; có, ai, đi: *està alguem que và*: aliquis ne est qui eat? ai là ai, ai nấy: *quemquer*: quisquis. chẳng có ai: *nao ha ninguem*: nullus est.

ai, vua hán ai đế: *nome do Rey da China em cuio tempo naceo Christo Nosso Senhor*: nomen Regis Sinarum qui regnabat cum natus est Christus

A

3. Alexandre de Rhodes' trilingual dictionary.

4. Quốc-ngữ' translation of Mendes Pinto's *Peregrination*.

5a. A piece of brick, Đại-la period.

5b. Base of a Cham pagoda in Mỹ-so'n.

6. A Cham pagoda in Nha-trang.

7. Thái-hoà Pavilion in the Imperial Palace in Huế.

8. Fans' dance performed by Cham girls.

9. Classical Vietnamese ballet performed in the Imperial Palace.

10. Dynastic Temple in Huê.

11. Mausoleum of Emperor Khải-định.

12. Memorial Ceremony for Emperor Quang-trung.

13. Gate of the Temple of General Lê Văn Duyệt in Gia-định near Saigon.

14. Vietnamese students in national costume, Aó-dài.